# The *Language* of Emotional Intelligence

The Five Essential Tools
for Building Powerful and
Effective Relationships

# The
# *Language* of
# Emotional
# Intelligence

## Dr. Jeanne Segal

Author of *Raising Your Emotional Intelligence*

### with Jaelline Jaffe, Ph.D.

New York   Chicago   San Francisco   Lisbon   London   Madrid   Mexico City
Milan   New Delhi   San Juan   Seoul   Singapore   Sydney   Toronto

The McGraw·Hill Companies

**Library of Congress Cataloging-in-Publication Data**

Segal, Jeanne, 1939–
    The language of emotional intelligence : the five essential tools for building powerful and effective relationships / by Jeanne Segal, with Jaelline Jaffe.
        p.    cm.
    ISBN-13: 978-0-07-154455-9 (alk. paper)
    ISBN-10: 0-07-154455-0 (alk. paper)
    1. Emotional intelligence.    2. Interpersonal communication.    3. Attachment behavior.    I. Jaffe, Jaelline Janice.    II. Title.

BF576.S43    2008
152.4—dc22                                                              2007045538

4  5  6  7  8  9  10  11  12  13  14  15  16  17  18  19  20  21    DOC/DOC    0

ISBN    978-0-07-154455-9
MHID      0-07-154455-0

Interior design by Think Design Group LLC

McGraw-Hill books are available at special quantity discounts to use as premiums and sales promotions or for use in corporate training programs. To contact a representative, please visit the Contact Us pages at www.mhprofessional.com.

This book is printed on acid-free paper.

*To the writers, Web-designers,*

*and Rotarians who make*

*helpguide.org a fitting memorial*

*to the life of our daughter*

*Morgan Leslie Segal*

*by helping millions enjoy*

*healthier, happier lives*

# Contents

# Acknowledgments

To Jaelline Jaffe for her many years of friendship and literary inspiration; my editor, Linda Laucella, for her calm and professional focus; my dream agent, Andrea Somberg, for her steadfast support; John Aherne, my editor at McGraw-Hill, for his insight and belief in me; and Robert, my playful, creative, and loving husband of fifty years, who makes me walk my talk.

# Introduction
## Emotionally Intelligent Communication Builds
## Emotionally Intelligent Relationships

Most people put their best foot forward in a new work setting or when looking to attract a mate, but often stumble while trying to keep their relationships rewarding. Emotional intelligence skills help you reach beyond initial good impressions to achieve more meaningful long-term relationships at home and at work.

Keeping a relationship productive and fulfilling requires a unique skill set that most of us have to learn. Conventional books and articles touting "relationship help" or "emotional intelligence at work" focus primarily on intellectual interventions for changing behavior, but they overlook the real source of our communication and relationship problems. Emotional memory and the perceptions we have of ourselves and others result from our very first relationship, known as the attachment bond. This book draws on new brain discoveries as the basis for developing skills that build your emotional intelligence. These skills help you keep all of your relationships productive and fulfilling.

## Why Is Emotional Intelligence So Important?

Emotion can override our thoughts and profoundly influence our behavior. Developing emotional intelligence skills helps us recognize, contain, and effectively communicate our emotions, as well as recognize the emotions of other people. These abilities have been proven to surpass high cognitive intelligence (IQ) in predicting success in all types of relationships, at home, at work, and in all other areas of our lives.

For example, when most people seek relationship help, they have problems in mind that they deem responsible for their conflicts—that is, their IQs have determined these problems to be the cause of their woes. What they don't realize is that usually more fundamental issues, which can be identified only by emotional intelligence, are creating and sustaining the difficulties they encounter in their relationships.

Consider these examples:

◇ Fred, who experienced emotional and physical pain early in life, is determined to keep his family together. His wife is threatening divorce. A bestselling book has outlined for Fred the steps he needs to take to change his behavior and to open up dialogue with his wife. Sadly, Fred cannot convince his wife of his good intentions, because most of his nonverbal, emotionally intelligent communication—the true language of love—conveys only *his* needs and ignores hers.

◇ Bonnie, whose parents died when she was an infant, is determined to put aside her depression, as well as her false expectations for emotional communication in her marriage. Men, the book suggests, aren't meant to be emotionally receptive; it's just not in their nature. Bonnie's husband is relieved to be off the hook. She, however, is anything but—her depression is worse and she has begun to suffer from irritable bowel syndrome.

◆ Joseph has been threatened by his colleagues to "go get help for your anger, or we are through." A local therapist refers him to an anger management program. There he learns to recognize some warning signs that he can anticipate to know when he might blow up and some techniques to cool off. But after a few successful "cool downs," Joseph and his management team become frightened when he goes into a rage over a minor disagreement.

◆ Allison gets a lot of attention for her good looks and sense of humor, but she never feels comfortable in her own skin. She dates a lot, but every time she finds someone she really likes, he stops calling after two or three dates. It never occurs to Allison that perhaps she does not know how to convey her interest. Instead, she finds a way to fault those who have disappointed her, instead of looking to herself as the cause of her problems.

◆ Alexis, whose mother was depressed when she was young, has a degree from one of the most prestigious law schools in the country. She normally looks and acts like someone in charge of herself, but she has an Achilles' heel. Alexis's inability to confront conflict has sidetracked her career. In spite of therapy, coaching, and good intentions to the contrary, she remains stuck and unable to advance.

In each example, the supposedly helpful relationship advice did not prove effective. Why? Because only the surface of the issues has been scratched; the *source* of the problem was never addressed.

## The Hidden Factors in Relationships and Communication

For decades, we have viewed relationship obstacles through a flawed lens, one that fails to capture a vivid picture of the real sources of connection and disconnection. This book looks at your communication skills under the microscope, revealing previously hidden answers to the things that go wrong. When we look at communication from a moment-to-moment perspective, as scientific brain technologies now enable us to do, we can see that what really keeps people engaged with one another lies beneath the surface. It is our nonverbal communication, the language of emotional intelligence, that keeps our relationships strong and healthy. While every relationship is unique, it has become apparent that there are five distinct parts to a communication process that builds emotional intelligence and helps inspire and sustain relationships.

We now know the following:

◇ The most powerful forms of communication contain no words and take place at a much faster rate than speech.
◇ One person's stress can block the communication process until both people again feel safe and can focus on one another.

◆ The adhesive that holds the communication process together is an emotional exchange triggered by primary biological emotions that include anger, sadness, fear, and joy.

◆ The ability to be playful translates into staying power. Mutual fun and joy enables relationships to thrive in the face of stressful and challenging situations.

◆ With the preceding nonverbal skills in place, conflict can be flipped into opportunity, building trust by quickly repairing instances of rupture.

## The Skills Needed for Emotionally Intelligent Communication

Taking full advantage of the cross-disciplinary scientific brain studies and discoveries of the past decade, this book provides you with the skills or tools that enable you to learn to communicate effectively with the people you work with and the people you love. These five essential skills define, empower, and guide your emotional intelligence in communication, giving you the means to create and sustain secure, successful, long-lasting relationships.

◆ **The elastic: high safety and low stress.** The capacity to regulate stress is the *elastic* that provides safety and gives rise to the ability to be emotionally available and engaged. Stress compromises this ability. The first step in communicating with emotional intelligence is recognizing when stress levels are out of control and returning ourselves and our colleagues or partners, whenever possible, to a relaxed and energized state of awareness.

◇ **The glue: exchange based on primary emotions.** The *glue* that holds the communication process together is the emotional exchange triggered by primary biological emotions that include anger, sadness, fear, joy, and disgust. These emotions, essential for communication that engages others, have often been numbed or distorted by misattuned early relationships, but they can and must be reclaimed and restored.

◇ **The pulley: wordless communication.** Nonverbal communication is the *pulley* of emotionally intelligent language that attracts the attention of others and keeps relationships on track. Eye contact, facial expression, tone of voice, posture, gesture, touch, intensity, timing, pace, and sounds that convey understanding engage the brain, influencing others much more than words alone can.

◇ **The ladder: pleasure in interactive play.** Playfulness and humor, the naturally high *ladder*, enable us to navigate awkward, difficult, and embarrassing issues. Mutually shared positive experiences also lift us up, strengthen our resolve, help us find inner resources needed to cope with disappointment and heartbreak, and give us the will to sustain a positive connection with our work and our loved ones.

◇ **The velvet hammer: conflict as opportunity for trust building.** The way we respond to differences and disagreements in home and work relationships can either create hostility and irreparable rifts or initiate the building of safety and trust—that's why it's a *velvet hammer*. The capacity to take conflict in stride and forgive easily is supported by our ability to manage stress, be emotionally honest and available, communicate nonverbally, and laugh easily.

Taken together, these crucial skills make us able to respond flexibly and appropriately in any situation. If this sounds revolutionary, *it is*. If it sounds too simple, *it is not*. Real change engages the brain and is an interactive process. Studies show that profound changes can be made in close relationships within three to nine months—a rebirth no longer than one's original creation.

## Why Is New Information Alone *Not* Enough for Change?

Our brains are uniquely structured to absorb information from people who are important to us. Human survival has always depended on the quality of our relationships with others. Physically vulnerable creatures that we are, we also need to adapt quickly; the ability to read and respond appropriately to the emotionally charged nonverbal cues coming from important others is a key to that success. All of this explains why the human brain throughout life is primed for new learning in emotionally laden and socially relevant contexts.

To learn in a manner that produces change (and not merely a glut of information), we need to engage the emotional centers of the brain in ways that connect us to others. There is a difference between *learning*—a process of intellectual absorption—and *changing*—a process of applying what we have learned to the varying circumstances in our lives. Change is a more complicated process involving brain integration than is data gathering.

Just reading this book won't be enough to raise your emotional intelligence. Not that it isn't a good start, but to change your work and home relationships you need to overcome distractions and dedicate time to acquiring and integrating the skills that permit emotional intelligence to flourish.

## Preparing for Change

How can you prepare for change?

◇ **Start by observing what gets in the way.** What gets in the way? What makes you too busy to dedicate quality uninterrupted time to exploring and practicing new skills? Most of us lead lives full of distraction. Our focused attention is constantly being interrupted, distracted, and absorbed by electronic gadgetry—cell phones, BlackBerries, e-mail, computers, and television. What will keep you from exploring and integrating the practices in the first part of this book that prime success for acquiring the skills in the second half of the book? Without indulging in self-criticism, just observe what you do with your time. Keeping a diary for a week or two might make you aware of how much time you have that you might want to use in other ways.

⬥ **Carve out some quality time for acquiring new skills.**
Dedicate from thirty to sixty minutes a day of quality time (in the earlier part of the day if you're a
morning person, in the evening if you're an evening person). Sometimes time can be acquired by
multitasking.

The emotional awareness exercise in the first half
of this book is in part a form of meditation. So if you
have already set aside a time to meditate, perhaps
this can be substituted. This exercise also accommo-
dates itself well to routine physical exercise, such as
solitary walking, when it is not necessary to remain
alert to traffic dangers.

⬥ **Motivate yourself every day.** Create a clear picture
in your mind's eye (your imagination) of what you
want to accomplish and why. Why do you want to
become more emotionally intelligent? What will you
gain that is important to you? Bring as much sensual awareness as possible into your process of imag-
ining what you want. See, smell, touch, taste, and
feel what being emotionally intelligent will be like
for you. Spend a little time before bed and after you
wake up in the morning dwelling on your good reasons for wanting to learn the skills that let you access
emotional intelligence.

⬥ **Be prepared for setbacks.** Change is always a "two
steps forward, one step back" process—expect that!
New ideas and new ways of being are programmed
into the brain alongside old information and practices. Eventually, there will be more new connections in the brain than old connections, but it takes

time and practice to build them. It also requires choice. During the process of exchanging new behavior for old behavior, it is not uncommon for the mind to present us with two differing possibilities—and it is up to us to choose the new over the old. This is where motivation comes in handy.

⬥ **Reward yourself.** Take time to appreciate all the hard work and the gains you are making. Notice the positive changes that are taking place in your life, and give yourself credit for these accomplishments. Acknowledge the effort you're making to change and the fact that it takes real courage to go where you have not gone before.

⬥ **Don't attempt change without the help and support of others.** You will need the support of family members, friends, colleagues, coworkers, or perhaps a counselor or therapist whom you can talk to about what you are doing and discovering. Talking about what you sense and feel will result in good feelings, but it will also integrate what you learn, giving it real sticking power. Besides talking to people who are close to you, trade off with someone you don't know as well but who also wants to raise his or her emotional intelligence. The two of you can take turns being the person who listens and the person who shares his or her experiences.

## Building Emotional Intelligence into All of Your Relationships

In this book you will find the following:

- Information to help you see yourself and others in a new light
- Guidelines to separate helpful from damaging communication
- Exercises to show you how to remain calm and focused, regardless of the circumstances
- Exercises to help you discover and improve your emotional awareness
- Ways to incorporate more playtime and joy into your relationships at work and at home
- Tips to turn conflict on its head, using it as an opportunity for building trust and steering clear of resentment

You will learn the following:

- The difference between talking and communicating
- How to reach deep into the mind and heart of another person
- How to have a positive impact on others without saying a word
- How to repair wounded feelings
- How to preserve trust and stoke the fires of admiration and attraction

## How Active Is Your Emotionally Intelligent Communication?

Most of us have problems dealing with difficult employees, coworkers, peers, or the people we care about in our private lives. The following quiz can give you a quick assessment of your basic emotional intelligence skills.

# Relationship Quiz
## Test Your Emotional Intelligence

Answer "usually," "occasionally," or "rarely" to the following questions:

1. I _____ sustain eye contact when speaking.

2. I _____ am comfortable with pauses when others are experiencing emotion.

3. I _____ sense when someone feels troubled before being told.

4. I _____ am comfortable with my feelings of sadness, joy, anger, and fear.

5. I _____ pay attention to my emotions when making decisions.

6. I _____ have no problem expressing my emotions to others.

7. I _____ can reduce my stress to a comfortable level.

8. I _____ enjoy laughing, playing, or kidding around.

9. I _____ don't feel threatened by disagreements.

Answering "usually" to most of these questions indicates that you have a good start toward emotionally intelligent communication in your relationships. Don't worry if you answered "occasionally" or "rarely." This book will help you build your emotional intelligence skills and improve your relationships at home and work.

# 1 | Why the Attachment Bond Matters

We look for reasons to explain why we didn't get the job or promotion we deserved; why the marriage, friendship, or relationship that meant so much to us failed; or why it's so hard to talk with our kids, family members, neighbors, or colleagues at work when we are not in agreement with them. We review our actions, wrack our brains, and search our souls, but rarely do we connect our frustrating and heartbreaking experiences to events that took place in our lives before we could think or speak. Yet during that time of wordless communication, the groundwork was laid for the success or failure in our future relationships. How did that process begin in the first place, and how does it eventually play itself out?

With these questions in mind, we can begin to understand why through no intention of our own, poor communication in our relationships results in frustration and
disappointment. But let's start at the beginning. Imagine
this conversation among four mothers, each with small
children:

"He's such a quiet baby—never gives me any trouble."

"Lucky you! Mine won't stop screaming; nothing I do
will make her stop. They say she's colicky—I say she's a
nightmare!"

"I can't leave this child with a sitter, let alone at preschool. She clings to me like Velcro—just won't let me go
without creating a huge scene. You'd think I wasn't ever
coming back . . . "

"Well, at least she acknowledges you. When I come to
pick up *my* kid from preschool, you'd think I was invisible. He acts like he doesn't even know I'm there!"

Most people probably would be concerned about the
screamer, questioning what is wrong with her and worry-
ing about her safety if the exhausted mother ever reaches
a breaking point. Many would also assume that the clingy
child is either too fragile or too spoiled. On the other
hand, it might be tempting to believe that a quiet baby
is a contented one or that a child who ignores his mother
is simply self-reliant and independent. On closer look,
however, we might see that the quiet baby seems to stare
into space, not making any contact with his mother. We
might notice that the child who seems unaware of his
mother is generally indifferent to her presence and seems
disconnected from her. Furthermore, if we checked this
preschool child's heart rate and blood pressure, we might
see that his nervous system mirrors that of the hysterical child.

If we followed these children throughout their school years, we might find that the quiet ones are easily ignored because they seem invisible. They might be labeled loners, socially inappropriate, or disinterested in learning. The noisy ones may be impossible to overlook, because they are disorderly and disruptive. Teachers or counselors might suspect these children of having attention deficit disorder (ADD) or attention deficit/hyperactivity disorder (ADHD). Following these children into adulthood, we would likely see them in difficult or unfulfilling relationships.

Recent developments in brain-imaging technology offer new explanations for these behaviors, allowing us to actually *see* and understand how experiences with other human beings affect the flow and function of information within our brains. Disruptions or changes in brain activity have been revealed through the use of electroencephalograms (EEGs), quantitative EEGs (QEEGs), positron emission tomography (PET) scans, single photon emission computed tomographies (SPECTs), and functional magnetic resonance imaging (MRI) scans. Fieldwork using still frames taken from videos set up in thousands of homes in many parts of the world has captured continuous, spontaneous interactions between infants and caretakers, validating the influence of the attachment bond on the nervous system and uncovering the secrets of the attachment bond.

Universally accepted by the scientific community, these advances have led to the conclusion that the *attachment* relationship plays a dominant role in the development of the brain, the individual, and his or her connection to others in the world. The security, or insecurity, of a child's early attachment relationship establishes the basis for:

- lifelong relationships with others
- a sense of security about exploring the world
- resilience to stress, adversity, disappointment, and loss
- the ability to recover from strong emotions, such as anger, anxiety, and sadness, and to balance one's emotions
- the ability to make sense of one's inner and outer worlds

## The Anatomy of a Relationship

What role does the attachment bond play in our adult relationships? Let's look in detail at a situation typical of many relationships that start out looking and feeling good, but fall apart in spite of their promising beginnings. As you read this story about Stephanie and Steven, notice your reactions:

- Do you have judgments about the people?
- Do you think one is right and the other is wrong?
- Has anything like this happened to you or anyone you know? If so, how did each person react?
- Why do you think these behaviors occurred on both sides?

### Stephanie and Steven: How Good Relationships Become Bad Relationships

The first time Stephanie saw Steven was in her office elevator. She was immediately attracted to him, loving the way his eyes crinkled when he joked with the man standing next to him. She learned from a friend that he worked in a different division within the corporation. When she saw him a week later at a company dinner, she got up the courage to ask him out.

To her delight, within the week they were dating. Stephanie felt that this one was different. "He's so right for me," she thought. They had romantic dinners, held hands at the movies, and went for long walks in the park. Together they laughed about their names: both had been called "Stevie" as children. It became their private term of endearment.

When she finally introduced Steven to her coworkers and relatives, everyone agreed that they made a great pair. Stephanie felt this one was it, the love of her life, the last she would ever want or need. Steven said and did all the right things. They talked about a future together, even playfully window-shopped for household items. Girlfriends pointed out bridal stores at the mall, and Stephanie's coworkers teased her about planning a shower.

In their second summer as a couple, the pair sailed on a romantic Caribbean cruise. They took long walks on sparkling beaches, holding hands and splashing in the clear turquoise water. They danced on the deck at midnight and kissed under the stars. Stephanie had never been happier.

A few days after their return, Steven was at Stephanie's kitchen table drinking coffee and Stephanie was musing over a recipe in the Sunday newspaper, when suddenly Steven announced, "I can't go to dinner at your sister's house next weekend."

Stephanie looked up from the paper and responded, "You can't?"

Instead of replying to her question, Steven went on as if she hadn't spoken, ". . . and I can't do this relationship anymore."

Stephanie sat paralyzed, almost unable to breathe. It was as if he had punched her in the stomach. She finally managed weakly, "What did you say?"

"I just can't go on like this."

"Like what? What's wrong, Steven?"

"I don't know," he said, staring into his coffee. "Something is just missing."

Despite Stephanie's fruitless questioning and tears, Steven gathered his toothbrush, clothes, and books. They traded house keys, and a short while later he was gone. Stephanie was in shock. She sobbed and wailed; her grief seemed bottomless.

For months after he left, Stephanie had trouble sleeping. She slept fitfully, had bad dreams, and dragged herself out of bed each morning to go to work. She played computer games, tried to read, and sometimes called night-owl friends. Even though friends listened and offered sympathy and suggestions, she began to feel guilty for troubling them and foolish for sounding like a broken record: "How could this happen? What went wrong? Why did I not see this coming? What do I do now?" She lost her appetite and lost weight. "Well," she tried to joke with herself, "that's one benefit!" But she knew she would rather have the weight back—along with the guy.

She wondered how much longer this pain would last and could not imagine ever trusting a man again. She was embarrassed to face the people in the office and became withdrawn and erratic in her work. For the first time in her life, she received a negative performance evaluation.

## What Went Wrong When It Seemed So Right?

What happened? How did a seemingly successful relationship fall apart so suddenly? What kind of person was Steven to behave so thoughtlessly, and is it possible that Stephanie really did not see this coming?

It would be easy to pass judgment on either of them, to write him off as a jerk or assume she had been too pushy and drove him away. But instead, let's look at these very human persons from the perspective of communication that succeeds or fails to connect us to others.

**Steven.** Steven was the youngest of three children, the son of Debra, a loving, somewhat older mother, and a father who loved his children but was forced to work out of state when his job was downsized. The timing couldn't have been worse. Debra was in the late stages of her pregnancy with Steven, and her husband's absence made her depressed. To make matters worse, Debra's mother, who had been ill for some time, died of cancer the year after Steven was born.

Although grieving the loss of her mother, Debra did her best to take good care of all three children. She threw birthday parties and attended parent conferences, and yet she was distracted by her own pain and loneliness. While she cared for her baby and met his physical needs adequately enough, Debra was emotionally inattentive. She rarely played with Steven and seemed to sleepwalk through the early months of his life.

To add to her distress, just a few months later Steven developed a serious infection and had to be hospitalized. As the sole caretaker for her three children, Debra was unable to stay with him during his week in the hospital. The sick little baby was overwhelmed, frightened by these strangers who seemed to be out to hurt him with their IV needles, noisy machines, and bustling interruptions of his restless sleep.

By the time Steven was two, his father was able to return home. Debra was relieved to have his emotional support. She recovered from the loss of her mother, and family life resumed a normal flow. Steven's older brothers, who had in essence grown up in a very different family, seemed secure and went on to develop emotionally engaging committed relationships with their wives. Steven grew up not knowing how to make friends with others. He had pals but no close friends, and he spent most of his time alone. At the same time, he was very uncomfortable with intense emotions such as sadness or anger, and he always "turned the volume down" on such feelings when they arose.

When Steven met Stephanie, he experienced an adrenaline rush—she was pretty and clever and seemed attracted to him. He looked forward to their time together and felt happier than he had ever been in his life. His previous marriage had ended badly, and he was aware that his inability to recognize his wife's emotions and communicate things that bothered him was a factor in the divorce. He promised himself that this time things would be different.

**Stephanie.** Stephanie had also been married before and desperately wanted this relationship to work out. She had dated a lot after her divorce and had been in a couple of long-term relationships but never felt deeply in love with any of her partners. Stephanie's family was close—eating dinner together nightly, visiting relatives on the weekend, and going to church together—but like Steven, Stephanie had her own emotional scars from childhood.

Stephanie's parents were not emotionally demonstrative, and while they clearly loved their kids, the focus of their attention was on academic achievement. Rational, unemotional behavior was the expected norm, and arguments or disagreements were firmly squelched. As a result, Stephanie had difficulty identifying her feelings, and fearing conflict, she was uncomfortable communicating her needs.

### How Can 1 + 1 = 0?

When Stephanie and Steven got together, they were excited and hopeful about their relationship. Over time they shared their dreams and began talking about the future. It certainly looked as though they were a committed couple. Caught up in the excitement of being with a positive, appreciative woman who shared his values, Steven pursued the relationship. Everyone who saw them got the impression that he was committed to his relationship with Stephanie.

But at the point where the newness of the relationship began to fade, Steven realized something was wrong. As he later said to Stephanie when he walked out, something was missing. The excitement he initially experienced with Stephanie faded, and he found his predicament impossible to discuss with her. While he continued to act as if everything was fine, in his private moments he felt otherwise:

- He was confused, anxious, and felt backed into a corner.
- He didn't experience a closeness with Stephanie, in spite of all their talk.

- He wondered what to say and what to do.
- He was uncertain about whether he really loved her.
- Most disturbing of all, he wondered if he was incapable of love and loyalty.

Meanwhile, encouraged by all the intimate words they had exchanged, Stephanie was carried away by the idea of the relationship. Although Steven now talked more, over time he actually had less to say about himself or about his feelings for her. Stephanie was so focused on the future that she became blind to things right in front of her, the nonverbal cues that something was wrong:

- The increasing lack of sustained eye contact between them
- The disappearance of small gestures of affection
- The loss of the intimate tone of voice he had used when they first met
- His "forgetfulness" about small promises
- The disappearance of the playfulness that had been an important part of their early relationship

By the time they went on their last vacation together, Steven already had long lost interest in her—he just hadn't told her yet.

## Wanting It to Work Isn't Enough

Despite their desire to be close, both Steven and Stephanie lacked the early life experiences and communication skills that would have enabled them to build a lasting relationship. Steven was disengaged, and Stephanie was anxious. Each one lacked the ability to be self-aware and self-revealing.

Adequate early relationships depend on an interactive communication process that conveys mutual recognition and understanding. It's about being seen and being known—being played with and *feeling* that your perceptions and emotions are observed and understood. Most of us know adults who say they were adored or even spoiled as children, yet still feel that their parents didn't really know or interact with them. Recent studies in child development suggest that the infant who doesn't have someone who laughs and plays with him or her, and whose caretaker cannot handle stress, rapidly resolve differences, or be emotionally available at least a third of the time, *is at risk of becoming an emotionally inadequate adult.* This largely unrecognized group comprises far more people than the group of those who experience obvious neglect and abuse.

If you don't know much about your childhood or how you were raised—or the childhood or parenting of other people in your life—how can you tell if this description applies? Deficient early relationships impact the infant brain in ways that can be seen in later behavior. As adolescents and adults, you may have noticed, or had others point out, such behaviors as the following:

◈ Failing to pick up on or respond appropriately to social cues
◈ Having less empathy and moral judgment than others seem to display
◈ Being anxious or edgy, or being withdrawn, spaced out, or shut down

- Being unable to repair rifts and surmount differences
- Being unable to calm and soothe yourself when you are feeling anxious or depressed
- Failing to be playful or to easily experience joy

If you didn't have the experience of adequate early relationships, here are some of the ways your adult relationships are probably affected. Take a deep breath and read these slowly. How many of them seem to reflect your experiences?

- You simply don't know what it means to be truly appreciated and understood.
- You don't know how to accept praise, caring, or goodwill when it is offered.
- You don't know how to be genuinely interested in or emotionally moved by other people.
- You don't know how to resolve differences without getting mad, tuning out, or splitting up.
- You don't know how to influence people.
- Your friends often seem to betray your trust.
- You have a constant need for control, power, and authority over others.
- You keep finding yourself in unsatisfying or unsuccessful relationships at home or at work.

In addition, when you compare yourself to others, you seem less able to bounce back after you suffer hurt or disappointment.

If you do identify with any of the preceding descriptions, hold on to the following thought: What has happened may not be anyone's fault—least of all yours!

# Is It Mother's Fault You're Messed Up?

Painful and isolating early life experiences can and do leave lasting imprints on our lives, but assigning blame usually is not the answer. The chaos, confusion, fear, and distrust caused by poor or inadequate early life experiences are likely to be handed down from one generation to the next. A mother who herself has not experienced *good enough* emotional communication or is emotionally unavailable for a good reason—grief, feeling overwhelmed, depression—probably will not be able to emotionally communicate with her infant, unless she has experienced repair. Mothers don't get up in the morning, look in the mirror, and say, "How can I disrupt my child's life today?" Usually caretakers do the best they can with the tools they have, but those tools just might be inadequate for the task.

It seems distressing to point to our earliest life experiences and find that some kind of neurological brain-circuitry disruption, usually unintentional, took place that may be damaging our current relationships, our work, and our happiness, and that we may unknowingly pass along these troubles to our children through our own underdeveloped abilities. Fortunately, thanks to what we have learned about brain development and secure attachment, we now know much more about what it takes to repair earlier damage.

## How Relationships Shape Brain Function

Stephanie, Steven, and the rest of us are born with brains that need positive interactive experiences to produce the states of balance necessary for healthy neurological development. Through the new brain-scanning technologies, science has documented that the brain is enormously plastic at birth and that it also retains some plasticity throughout life. Although we used to believe the brain was incapable of change once we reached adulthood, we now know that's not true. According to UCLA child psychiatrist and developmental specialist Daniel J. Siegel, "At birth the brain is the most undifferentiated organ in the body with a plasticity that enables it to create new circuitry throughout life. This capacity for structural and functional change . . . never really ceases and the greatest impetus to change is *relationship*."

Like a science fiction movie come true, the use of brain-scanning techniques allows us to *see* the following:

◇ The brain can continually produce new neural pathways even as old ones are dying, no matter our age.
◇ Interactive experience—that is, communications with other people—rather than genetics plays the more dominant role in shaping and reshaping the structure and function of the brain and in determining personal and interpersonal response and behavior.

## Communication That Alters Brain Structure and Function

Why is it that we can often sense the insincerity of someone's words in casual conversation or even that of a speaker who is earnestly giving a presentation? This, in essence, is the heart of emotional intelligence. Our brains are attuned to "read" the subtle nonverbal messages of emotional intelligence that contrast with the spoken word. Unspoken signals are triggered by deeply felt emotions that register in facial expressions, timing, movements, and tone of voice. These nonverbal messages—whether calming and energizing, or negative and manipulative—are much more significant and persuasive than words. Physical and emotional expression is what draws people to us or makes them avoid us, and the new research and technology explain why.

At birth a person's brain is so socially attuned that wordless communication, independent of genetic factors, is primarily responsible for shaping development. The brain's remarkable plasticity at this point—the ability to change both structure and function—sets a lifelong template for thoughts, feelings, and behavior. Moreover, because the brain *remains flexible throughout life*, nonverbal forms of communication retain the capacity to create continuous changes.

### Attachment and How It Affects Relationships

The brain at birth is programmed to connect us to one very significant person. How we relate to that special someone is determined by our emotional intelligence—our nonverbal communication—and will in fact determine how we relate to other people later in life. The attachment bond formed *back then* was our first experience in communication and sets the stage for our ability to communicate in all future relationships. People who experienced confusing, frightening, or broken emotional communications early in life often grow into adults who have difficulty understanding what they and others experience emotionally. In turn, this will greatly limit their ability to accurately assess and successfully participate in relationships.

The psychological concept of "attachment" is gaining in recognition, both in the professional and popular press. In the 1950s, English psychiatrist John Bowlby first articulated attachment theory. His premise was that attachment, the relationship between infant and primary caretaker, is responsible for the following:

◆ Shaping the success or failure of future intimate relationships
◆ Aiding or hindering our abilities to focus, be conscious of our feelings, and calm ourselves
◆ Enabling us to enjoy being ourselves and to find satisfaction in being with others
◆ Enabling us to rebound from misfortune

Later social scientists, led by Mary Ainsworth, videotaped spontaneous interactions between parents and their young children. They analyzed thousands of still frames from these videos and observed "secure" and "insecure" attachments based on their observations of the subtle nuances between a caretaker and child, specifically how a child reacted to a caretaker when the caretaker left and then reentered a room. In a successful ("secure") attachment, emotionally attuned communication and interaction was clearly recognized as mutual connection and understanding, whereas in a problematic ("insecure") attachment, communication efforts did not achieve the same effect. These social scientists discovered that a positive attuned brain-altering relationship is based on five distinct parts of the communication process that continue to inspire and sustain the desire for intimacy: mutual regulation, nonverbal communication, emotional exchange, interactive play, and willingness to readily resolve differences. Even mothers who love and care for their children can fail to provide their offspring with good attachment experiences if they don't play with them, don't emotionally communicate with them, or frequently misread, misunderstand, or ignore their baby's cues.

The experience of connection or disconnection described by *attachment* profoundly shapes our expectations, behaviors, and ability to communicate positively in important relationships throughout our lives. It also provides road maps that help us see where we have been, where we are now, and what we can do to be where we want to be—now and in the future.

# 2 How the Attachment Bond Creates Trust in Ourselves and Others

A lthough falling in love is sometimes easy, half of all first marriages end in divorce. Even more astounding is the fact that two-thirds of second marriages also fail. And many people stay in marriages that have lost the joy, interest, and excitement needed to make the relationship permanently fulfilling. Advice usually given by marriage therapists, magazine articles, or some self-help books may temporarily relieve the *symptoms* of your relationship problems, but following that advice doesn't usually *change* the flawed attachment-based interactive processes that continue to undermine trust, self-worth, mutual understanding, and affection.

Researchers have found that successful adult relationships depend on the persons' emotional intelligence—on their ability to:

◈ manage stress and adversity
◈ stay tuned in with emotions
◈ use communicative, emotionally intelligent body language
◈ be playful in a mutually engaging manner
◈ be readily forgiving, relinquishing grudges

## Mark and Cheryl: A Seemingly Unsuited Couple

Mark and Cheryl met professionally when Mark was in the midst of a painful, prolonged divorce that he had attempted to avoid. After years of trying to understand why his wife treated him with contempt, Mark had discovered that she was having an affair, which she had no intention of ending. But when he finally filed for divorce, she made it quite clear that she didn't want to end their marriage, because she was happy with the arrangement as it was.

Cheryl, who was in her early forties—as was Mark when they met—had never been married, despite having been in several long-term relationships. She was adopted as a baby by parents who had converted to a religion (when she was an adult) that they insisted she embrace. Unable to do so, Cheryl became estranged from her parents and was now alone, without family in the world. Fiercely independent, curious, and successful in the real estate field (the same field as Mark), Cheryl had recently taken up a serious interest in acting.

Their beginnings were on a note of friendship. Although Mark did feel a strong attraction for Cheryl, he also recognized and respected the fact that she was not looking for romance. Between her work and her passion for acting, she had little available time for him—at first, only every few weeks. Still, when they did get together, each found the other to be a ready listener, and there was a real emotional exchange between them that often included laughter, as well expressions of pain, sadness, and frustration. Having come from a family that talked openly about their feelings, including their vulnerable feelings, Mark felt warmed by Cheryl's attentiveness and acceptance. Encouraged by his emotional openness and interest in her, Cheryl revealed more and more about what moved and motivated her. Cheryl found herself increasingly looking forward to being with Mark, and Mark, who had always been rather staid in his ways, found himself being influenced by her interest and excitement about so many things. He even began taking an acting class because he was curious to see why she found it to be so meaningful—and he really liked it, to the complete surprise of his friends and family. Cheryl was also interested in health and fitness, another new subject that Mark pursued and enjoyed because of her.

Little by little Cheryl found herself drawn into her relationship with Mark. No one had ever made her feel so known, heard, respected, and appreciated. She became increasingly attracted to him, and she missed him when they were not together. By the time their lovemaking began in earnest, both felt known and valued. Their intimacy was mutually fulfilling, but so was the time they shared before and after lovemaking. Now married, Mark and Cheryl remain joyful confidants, curious explorers, and lovers.

The difference between the way Mark and Cheryl's relationship progressed and that of Steven and Stephanie from Chapter 1 is defined by the quality of their communication. Mark and Cheryl enjoyed an emotional interchange that mirrored good attachment and high emotional intelligence. Their communication is based on:

◆ self-awareness
◆ a willingness to be self-revealing
◆ the capacity to listen to the emotional content of what is being said—*and to be moved by it*
◆ the ability to express one's own emotions
◆ a willingness to be emotionally moved and affected by the other—to change as a result of the relationship

Knowledge of the living brain and the role that attachment plays in shaping it has given us a new science for understanding why even smart people may have great difficulty communicating well with the most important people in their lives—both personally and professionally. Previously, we could only speculate as to why important relationships never evolved or why they disappeared, disintegrated, or became contentious. But thanks to new insights into brain development, we now understand what it takes to help build and sustain productive, meaningful work and home relationships. Cross-disciplinary research in neurology, psychiatry, biology, genetics, and psychology offers clear evidence of how and why the attachment bond continues to influence our lives. Out of this research comes the awareness that humans are incredibly social beings constantly shaped by the influences of important others and especially by our first love relationship.

For better or worse, the infant brain is profoundly impacted by the attachment bond—a baby's first love relationship. When a baby's primary caretaker can manage personal stress, calm the infant, communicate through emotion, share joy, and forgive readily, the young child's nervous system becomes securely attached. With a successful attachment relationship in tow, the child will be self-confident, trusting, and comfortable in the face of conflict. As an adult, he or she will prove to be flexible, creative, hopeful, and optimistic.

A secure attachment bond formed with a primary caretaker shapes our ability to:

◇ feel safe
◇ develop meaningful interpersonal connections with other people
◇ explore the world
◇ deal with stress and adversity
◇ recover from disappointment and loss
◇ balance emotions
◇ experience comfort and security
◇ make sense of our lives
◇ have positive memories and expectations of love and other close relationships

Every person's attachment occurs in a unique way. Primary caretakers don't have to be perfect; they can even miss opportunities for emotional attunement more often than not. But when the attachment bond fails to provide sufficient structure, recognition, understanding, safety, and mutual accord, children such as Stephanie and Steven develop insecure forms of attachment, such as anxiety or distancing.

## Insecure Attachment Affects Future Relationships

Misattunement with the one person the brain recognizes as our link to life alters the anatomy of our nervous system. In the future, when we are with someone who is important to us, our experience will likely include painful and confusing memories and expectations. These imprints will shape our ability to trust and invest in new relationships. Stephanie, for example, was a loved child but never learned to communicate her wants and needs or to express emotions in her logical, rational family. Steven also was loved but was unintentionally subjected to fear and abandonment by his life circumstances, leaving him anxious and fearful of others. Without an understanding of each other's individual histories, their relationship was almost ensured to be difficult to sustain.

Insecurity takes root when the attachment bond fails to provide a child with sufficient structure, recognition, understanding, safety, and mutual accord. It is as likely to stem from isolation or loneliness as it is from abuse. These insecurities may lead us to do the following:

- **Tune out and turn off.** If our parent is unavailable and self-absorbed, as children we may get lost in our own inner worlds, avoiding any close, emotional connections. As adults, we may become physically and emotionally distant in relationships.
- **Remain insecure.** If we have a parent who is inconsistent or intrusive, we likely will become anxious and fearful, never knowing what to expect. As adults, we may be available one moment and rejecting the next.
- **Become disorganized, aggressive, and angry.** When our early needs for emotional closeness go unfulfilled or when our parent's behavior is a source of disorienting terror, problems are sure to follow. As adults, we may not love easily and we are insensitive to the needs of our partner.
- **Develop slowly.** Such delays manifest themselves as deficits and result in subsequent physical and mental health problems, and often, social and learning disabilities.

## What Conditions Can Lead to Insecure Attachment?

The following are major causes of insecure attachment:

- **Physical neglect:** poor nutrition, insufficient exercise, and neglect of medical issues
- **Emotional neglect or emotional abuse:** little attention paid to the child; little or no effort to understand the child's feelings; verbal abuse

- **Physical abuse:** physical violence, sexual violation
- **Separation from primary caregiver:** rupture due to illness, death, divorce, adoption
- **Changes in primary caregiver:** succession of nannies
- **Frequent moves or placements:** constantly changing environment
- **Traumatic experiences:** serious illnesses or accidents
- **Maternal depression:** withdrawal from maternal role due to isolation, lack of social support, hormonal problems
- **Maternal addiction to drugs or alcohol:** maternal responsiveness reduced by mind-altering drugs
- **Undiagnosed painful illness:** conditions such as colic, ear infections, and so on
- **Lack of attunement or harmony between mother and child:** differences in temperament between child and parents
- **Young or inexperienced mother:** lack of parenting skills, including attachment skills

These insecure relationships are not necessarily pure in their forms and may overlap one another. So to survive, the brain adjusts to insecurity in the attachment bond by developing in less-than-optimal ways. This readjustment to accommodate survival in less-than-secure situations, in turn, affects the way we feel about ourselves and how we communicate with others in the future.

Symptoms of insecure attachment that carry over into adulthood include the following:

- **Low self-esteem:** needy, clingy, or "I don't need anyone" pseudoindependent behavior

◇ **Inability to deal with stress and adversity:** lack of self-control and inability to regulate feelings and emotions

◇ **Inability to develop and maintain relationships:** alienation from and opposition to parents, family members, and authority figures

◇ **Antisocial attitudes and behaviors:** aggression and violence

◇ **Difficulty with trust:** uncomfortable with intimacy and affection

◇ **Negativity:** hopeless, pessimistic view of self, family, and society

◇ **Lack of empathy:** absence of compassion and remorse

◇ **Behavioral and academic problems:** speech and language problems, difficulty learning

◇ **Incessant chatter:** can't listen or be still

◇ **Depression:** apathy, disinterest

◇ **Susceptibility to chronic illness:** always ill

◇ **Obsession with food:** hordes, gorges, refuses to eat, hides food

The list is long enough to include relationship difficulties that just about everyone has had at home or at work at one time or another. The problem is in degrees: can we as adults develop a successful, fulfilling, sustained relationship with at least one significant person, or are relationships perpetually strained, broken, or avoided? What matters most, however, is that because of the brain's lifelong flexibility—another monumental recent neurological discovery—there is always the potential for creating new patterns of communication based on the kinds of experiences observed in *secure* attachments. Especially hopeful are studies of couples with only one secure partner, which indicate that the positive influence of that partner in the relationship can lead to the development of greater security in the insecure partner.

## What Attachment Insight Tells Us About Our Love Relationships

The powerful life-altering impact of our first love relationship has surprising things to teach us about our adult love relationships. First, this primary relationship is based entirely on emotionally charged wordless forms of communication. Although newborn infants can't talk, reason, or plan, they are well equipped to get their own needs met. The parts of their brains that immediately come on line after birth have to do with survival, and survival has to do with emotional awareness. They don't *know* what they need; they *feel* what they need and communicate accordingly. When an infant is able to communicate its needs to someone who has the ability to use her or his own feeling state to grasp the baby's meaning and to respond sensitively, something life-altering and wonderful occurs. It's the language of emotional intelligence at its purest and best.

First love relationships teach us:

◇ Love isn't enough to ensure a strong and lasting love relationship—trust, shared joy, and emotionally fulfilling communication are equally essential.

- Good intentions and willpower aren't enough either—the resources for creating trust, emotional understanding, and joy are also needed.
- Relationships have the power to influence the way the brain develops.
- Knowing what is responsible for success or failure in early love relationships offers us a new model for attracting and sustaining relationships that grow more meaningful and rewarding over time. *Misattuned relationships can be repaired.* Even individuals who lack positive attachment skills can learn to develop and apply these skills in intimate and other emotionally close relationships.

## How Attachment Insight Applies to Work Relationships

A relationship with an emotional charge can trigger emotional memories and any behavior attached to these memories. When our boss or a coworker dismisses or criticizes us, we can be instantly drawn into the emotions and sensations we felt so long ago. If we haven't learned how to calm and soothe these feelings, they can get the better of us, disrupting our work to a degree that is disabling. Even more important, if like Stephanie or Steven we are unaware of our needs, we may never be able to find fulfillment in what we do. No matter how smart we are or how ably we perform our duties, we can't escape the interpersonal nature of most work environments. The more skilled we are at communicating not only our thoughts but also our feelings, the greater likeliness there is of finding and perpetuating meaningful and rewarding work relationships.

People who experience success in their work:

◇ know what they need
◇ can capture and hold the attention of others
◇ can repair upsets quickly and easily
◇ can communicate compassion
◇ are a pleasure to be around
◇ easily ask for what they want—but don't expect to always get what they want
◇ aren't afraid to disagree

### Allen: A Man Who Could Accept Unflattering Words

In the midst of a creative surge, Allen was completely revising and upgrading a major website that he had created. Because he needed to accomplish a lot in a very short turnaround period, he hired two talented young tech employees. The three of them worked together very closely and productively day and night for several months. Then Allen, who was much older than the new recruits, began to lose steam, despite his ongoing passion, excitement, and dedication to the work. Allen was a terrific boss—direct, emotionally open about his feelings, funny, and, best of all, appreciative of his employees' efforts and accomplishments. Nonetheless, he began to get on their nerves as he stood over them, watching their every move. Fatigued at this point, Allen's role consisted mostly of pointing out what wasn't going to work, which put a damper on the creative process of the others. Being creative himself, Allen understood that the freedom to make mistakes is crucial during the creative process, but he was running on one cylinder.

The young people, buoyed by Allen's previous praise and his emotional openness, took a leap of faith and decided to trust him with the truth that he was now getting in their way. Because their working relationship with Allen had always been based on honesty and goodwill, they suggested to him that if he left them alone for the rest of the day they could be more productive. To Allen's credit, he was aware of his physical fatigue and able to recognize that it was clouding his ability to be a positive, contributing member of the team. He laughingly acknowledged that he was tired and went home early. As a result, when Allen went into the office the next morning, he found that the work on his website had progressed nicely without him. Ultimately, the incident further facilitated the highly productive working relationship of his creative team.

## We're Not Stuck with Our Limitations

Relationship-destroying patterns of communication brought about through inadequate early relationships, isolation, abuse, or neglect can be changed. *We are not lifelong prisoners of our childhood experiences.* Our brains remain receptive to change—especially in contexts where feelings and emotions flow from moment to moment. Change is a social phenomenon that we can orchestrate with the help of supportive friends, loved ones, and coworkers. New neural patterns can be created throughout life in relationships that mirror those of successful attachment. Just as the damage created by an inadequate early relationship can be seen on brain scans, improvements can also be seen. In the following chapters, we'll explore just how we can begin to facilitate this change through the language of emotional intelligence.

The following attachment styles and parental styles, along with the ways they may be seen in adult relationships, give us significant clues to where we may be starting out and offer a new glimpse into creating fulfilling love and work relationships, by providing the keys to identifying and rectifying relationships that are on the rocks.

| ATTACHMENT STYLE | PARENTAL STYLE | ADULT RELATIONSHIPS |
|---|---|---|
| Secure | Aligned or attuned with the child | Able to create meaningful relationships; empathetic, appropriate boundaries |
| Avoidant | Unavailable or rejecting | Avoids closeness, emotional connection; distant, critical, rigid, intolerant |
| Ambivalent | Inconsistent and sometimes intrusive parent communication | Anxious and insecure; controlling, blaming; erratic, unpredictable, sometimes charming |
| Disorganized | Ignore or don't see the child's needs; behavior is frightening or traumatizing | Chaotic, insensitive, explosive, abusive; untrusting even while craving security |
| Reactive | Extremely unattached or displaying a disrupted nervous system | Cannot establish positive relationships; often misdiagnosed |

The following summary of the elements of attuned, disrupted, and repaired attachment helps you see how well-acquainted you are with emotionally intelligent communication. The five nonverbal skills you need to create and repair attachment and improve emotionally intelligent language will be discussed in Chapter 8, where you will have the opportunity to identify your strengths and weaknesses in regard to each.

| EMOTIONALLY INTELLIGENT COMMUNICATION | DISRUPTED COMMUNICATION | REPAIRED COMMUNICATION |
|---|---|---|
| ◆ Mother and infant nonverbal communication is activated by brain resonance. <br><br> ◆ Primary caretaker notices, understands, and responds appropriately to felt emotions. <br><br> ◆ When disconnection or misunderstanding does occur, it is quickly repaired. <br><br> ◆ Feeling safe results in the ability to understand the self and to relate well to others. | ◆ Primary caretaker is distracted, depressed, or emotionally unavailable. <br><br> ◆ Emotional communication from the infant is misinterpreted or ignored, leading to neural disruption. <br><br> ◆ Disruption occurs repeatedly, with little or no repair, resulting in insecurity and mistrust. <br><br> ◆ Lack of safety leads to the inability to establish healthy relationships. | ◆ Sharing feelings with someone who receives and accurately reflects emotional experiences. <br><br> ◆ Taking in the trusted other's experience of you. <br><br> ◆ Retrieving and reconnecting with true biological feelings of sadness, anger, fear, shame, and joy. <br><br> ◆ Verbally acknowledging changes and positive feelings; greater success and satisfaction in this and other relationships. |

# 3 Why Stress Cripples Effective Communication

The first step in preparing for emotionally intelligent communication is *recognizing* when our own stress levels, or those of our partners or our colleagues, are out of control. Unrecognized stress responses play such an important role in our abilities to communicate effectively that they can undermine even the strongest love and work relationships.

## How Stress Challenges Relationships at Home and Work

Stress can weaken relationships by crippling our abilities to:

◇ accurately read another person's nonverbal
communications
◇ hear what someone is really saying
◇ be aware of our own feelings
◇ be in touch with our deep-rooted needs
◇ communicate our needs clearly

Although every individual and every person's emotional makeup is different, it is useful to consider the following typical examples of how stress affects relationships:

◇ Irene has a new job with much more pressure and hasn't been sleeping well. She is cranky when she gets home and in no mood to listen to Alex talk about his day. No matter how hard she tries to be interested and listen, she can't stay focused. Alex feels hurt and as a result, goes out by himself, leaving Irene home alone.
◇ Norm is under a lot of pressure at school but doesn't want to break his date with Kristy. Even though he usually enjoys her playful kidding and finds it amusing, tonight it infuriates him and he explodes. Kristy is hurt. She has no idea why Norm is behaving in a way that is so unlike him.
◇ Ben, stressed to the point of exhaustion after too many days of overscheduling and multitasking, has collapsed in front of the TV, missing a critical after-hours call from work.
◇ Mary Alice and her best friend have such a heated argument that she heads to the mall to cool off and distract herself. There, she loses track of the time and is a no-show for dinner with Sam, who is com-

pletely in the dark about what's going on and thinks he has done something wrong.

◆ Terri is feeling so overwhelmed by debt that she cannot maintain her focus at work and just goes through the motions, accomplishing nothing—a fact that does not escape the notice of her boss and is jeopardizing her job.

◆ Stephanie is so jumpy and agitated that no one at work wants to be near her. She thinks her colleagues don't like her, but they are avoiding the tension she radiates.

In these examples, Norm, Mary Alice, and Stephanie appear hot, angry, and agitated—hyperaroused; Irene, Ben, and Terri seem spacey, withdrawn, or depressed—hypoaroused. Although a person's hyper (i.e., overexcited) behavior may appear to be completely different and even opposite from a person's "hypo" (i.e., underexcited) stress responses, in actuality they produce similar disruptions in the nervous system: their internal (within their bodies) responses to stress can be identical. In fact, heart rates and blood pressure can be even higher in those who are withdrawn than in those who are enraged.

## How Stress Affects the Nervous System and Undermines Relationships

For most people, experiencing stress is so routine that it becomes a way of life. In fact, not all stress is bad; it can motivate us and give us the incentive to accomplish the things we want or need to do. But when stress is out of balance or overwhelming, it has negative effects on our nervous systems, limiting our abilities to think clearly and creatively or to act in ways that are emotionally intelligent and beneficial for our relationships. This creates situations such as the following:

◇ **One person's upset can easily trigger another's anxiety, leading to escalating disconnection in communications.** Patricia had a new baby, and she often came to work a little tired. But she loved her challenging and rewarding job. Amy, the company's bookkeeper, envied Patricia's family (her devoted husband and adorable children). But she also felt that Patricia got more attention and appreciation at work than she did and resented the fact that they both received the same salary—even though Patricia hadn't worked for the company as long.

   Amy made no effort to conceal her disgruntled feelings. She avoided Patricia as if she were contagious and barely looked at her, despite that their offices were adjacent. In the beginning, Patricia's natural confidence kept her from being drawn into Amy's negative energy, but with the added fatigue of juggling a new baby and work, she felt increasingly anxious at the office.

◇ **Negative memories from past relationships flood us, adding to the upsets of the moment.** From a background of poverty and abuse, James rose through the ranks to successfully head a large financial institution. Normally charming and gregarious, his weak spot was criticism. Being criticized triggered a torrent of memories that left him feeling fearful, humiliated, and enraged. Still, he was good enough at what he did to hang on to his job for many years. But one day when he lost it in front of his board of directors because of a minor criticism, he also lost their respect and eventually, his job.

◇ **When we are overwhelmed by stress, our abilities to pay attention to others and ourselves are greatly compromised.** Kay, a successful businesswoman and community volunteer, headed up a committee that was in charge of designing and building a new youth center. Normally Kay was sensitive to others, as well as competent and levelheaded, but her home life was in turmoil. Her father had recently died, and both her husband and brother were diagnosed with serious diseases. Kay's response to this stress was to numb her emotions and focus intellectually on problems that needed to be solved. But by avoiding her emotions, she also failed to read the nonverbal signals coming from other committee members, who disagreed with her choice of architect for the project. Her failure to understand their concerns, along with her desire to quickly complete the work, unwittingly created an adversarial relationship with some committee members. Because of her confusion and frustration with the process, she became so overwhelmed that she resigned her leadership position. The remaining committee members subsequently chose an inexperienced architect who designed a building that cost far more to build than was budgeted.

## The Most Common Stress Response Patterns

Our nervous systems react differently to situations that are, or are perceived to be, overwhelming, isolating, confusing, or threatening. No two people are wired exactly the same, but Dr. Connie Lillas, a child development expert from Los Angeles, uses the analogy of driving a car to describe the three most common ways people respond to stress:

- **Foot on the gas:** a heated, angry, in-your-face response, where the person is agitated and can't sit still
- **Foot on the brake:** a shut-down, depressed, withdrawn response, where the person exhibits little energy or emotion
- **Foot on both:** a tense and still response, where the person's eyebrows may be raised, eyes wide open, shoulders tight and lifted; the person is frozen, can't get going, and can't accomplish anything

Jack and Tess love and genuinely care about one another, but neither feels truly loved by the other, and they have struggled for years to live well together. Typical of the way they relate is what happened one evening when Tess asked Jack to meet her for dinner at a hotel restaurant in another part of town, where she was conducting a business meeting. Jack agreed with enthusiasm but got lost driving to the hotel. (Jack is very bright but has attention deficit disorder [ADD] and easily gets lost.) Feeling ashamed and embarrassed—and fearing Tess's wrath—Jack zoned out and failed to call Tess to tell her what had happened. After waiting for an hour, Tess was furious and ate dinner alone (without calling Jack to see what had happened, because she was certain that once again he had flaked out on her—another sign of his disregard for her feelings). By the time they met up at home later that evening, each had spiraled down into a numbing depression that left them both mute and unable to communicate.

## When to Wait Before Acting

Is your foot on the gas or the brake internally? Are you overwhelmed to the point that you feel out of control? If the answer to questions like these is yes, it's time to stop and wait until you steer yourself back into balance. As you become a stress-busting detective, you will learn that:

◇ The first principle for improving relationships is to recognize an imbalance in yourself. Then it also will be much easier to recognize an imbalance in others.
◇ The second principle is to wait until your balance is restored before attempting any sort of constructive communication process. Proceeding from a state of imbalance will likely make matters worse.

## Recognizing Particular Stress Response Patterns

An inability to recognize that each person may have different stress patterns can result in seemingly insurmountable difficulties in communication, creating misunderstandings and distance in relationships.

While there can be some crossover, generally each individual responds to stress with a discernible pattern of either overexcitation (hyper) or underexcitation (hypo). This means that some commonly recommended stress-relief techniques "for everyone" may have no effect at all or might even make matters worse. For example, if your response to stressful situations is to become depressed or withdrawn, you need to do things that stimulate rather than relax you.

The most effective method of stress relief for each individual depends on the person's particular stress pattern. But in general, there are two approaches to relieving a person's stress response, depending on whether the person tends to become overexcited or underexcited:

1. A person who becomes angry or agitated responds to efforts that help calm and soothe, such as those that will slow down the person's breathing and create relaxing sensations.
2. A person who becomes withdrawn, spaced-out, or depressed responds best to stimulating activities, such as strenuous exercise, creating sensations that stimulate and energize the nervous system.

## Recognizing Stress Improves Relationships

No one is always perfectly balanced. Stress is an equal-opportunity hazard, upsetting everyone's equilibrium from time to time. When we walk into a situation tired and irritated, coming face-to-face with an equally stressed-out loved one or colleague, we rarely have the option to take time out for a nap or meditation. Still, our bodies and minds can quite quickly and efficiently bring stress into balance. To balance stress, however, you must do the following:

1. First realize that you are stressed and recognize your individual stress response.
2. Then learn the methods to quickly and dependably regulate your nervous system, bringing it back into balance.

There is a supportive relationship between the ability to recognize stress and becoming emotionally aware. As you become more aware of your emotions and other feelings in your body, you will also become more aware of your stress triggers. Learning to bring down your stress level enables you to be more fully engaged in the array of emotions that contribute to open, honest, and genuine interactions in relationships.

## Learning to Manage Stress Helps Relationships

It is often apparent when stress has a negative effect on our personal and work relationships. But sometimes a person's external presentation (i.e., behavior) covers up the internal reality (i.e., feelings inside)—even to him- or herself. Learning to recognize and manage stress and to stay calm and focused sets the stage for the following:

◇ **Internal focus.** This enables us to pay closer attention to how we are feeling inside while meeting the demands of others in our lives. As an example, Jack's desire to help others makes him popular, but by developing bleeding ulcers, he has learned the hard way that giving too much to others creates problems for himself. By paying more attention to his internal state of energy and focus, he recognizes when it's time to shift the focus from others back to himself. Taking care of himself and his own needs actually allows Jack to give more of himself to the people and projects he cares about most.
◇ **Mind/body unity.** This integrates communication so that our words and body language convey the same

message. Bright eyes, a soft face, a gentle tone, an easy pace, and relaxed shoulders all communicate what we cannot when we are agitated, fearful, withdrawn, or depressed.

◆ **Recognizing inappropriate behaviors in our relationships.** This allows us to feel "just right" and stable, enhancing our abilities to become more aware of detrimental knee-jerk behaviors in others and ourselves. Maintaining internal balance helps us maintain focus—even when the other person becomes angry or defensive.

◆ **Having energy to spare.** Lacking internal controls can leave us drained, but learning to calm and soothe ourselves gives us the ability to quickly adjust, regaining our internal balance. Lots of energy is needed to effect change, but this energy isn't available when our nervous systems are constantly in a state of flux.

# Remaining Calm and Focused Under Stress

Many of us, spending so much of our lives in an unbalanced state, have probably forgotten what it feels like to be fully relaxed and alert. We can see that "just right" inner balance in the face of a happy baby, so full of joy that it makes everybody else regain perspective. For adults, feeling just right equals energy and alertness, and focus and calm, and being with such a person just feels right.

Staying calm and focused under stress is characterized by the following:

◇ **Feelings of control.** The ability to harness or unleash our energy at will and appropriately take charge in any situation gives us confidence in ourselves.

◇ **Heightened sensory awareness.** Calming and invigorating, it's acquired through both internal and external sources. Colors are brighter, scents and tastes more intense, sounds clearer, and touch more penetrating. An overall awareness of our bodies even translates to a sense of grace.

◇ **Trust in others.** A working knowledge that people can be dependable and caring and that we can feel safe in their company is invaluable.

◇ **Curiosity.** We need a sense that the world is there to be explored. We have a desire, infused with hope and promise, to uncover the unknown.

◇ **Playfulness.** Experiencing unbridled joy and laughter, and finding childlike joy in simple, noncompetitive activities are essential.

◇ **Creativity.** When delight in discovery enters the intellectual realm, work becomes playful exploration, as our thoughts break free from constraints.

◇ **Ability to rebound from setbacks.** Emotional resilience makes it possible not only to shoulder losses but also to bounce back and score victories.

◇ **Ability to attend to self-needs, as well as the needs of others.** We can't please all the people all the time, but that doesn't mean we need to walk through this world alone. We have it within each of us to be flexible, work collaboratively with others, and be both leaders and followers.

## Kristin: The Young Woman Who Confronted Her Boss

Kristin was thrilled to get the job. It was a dream come true to be hired right out of school and be paid while earning hours for her psychology license. With friendly, helpful, and very experienced coworkers, she admired everyone in the office, especially her supervisor, Barbara, who was very open and receptive to Kristin's ideas. Barbara even allowed Kristin, despite being a rank beginner, to start two new groups at the agency.

On Kristin's day off, as she was about to leave home for a weekly morning tennis game, she received a call from the office to help locate some files that no one could find. Since the office was near the tennis court, she offered to pop in for a minute to help. At the office, Kristin was bent over looking through a stack of files, wearing a short tennis dress, when Barbara entered the room. Instead of being grateful that Kristin had come in on her day off to lend a hand, Barbara hit the roof, yelling, "How could you come into the office dressed like that?" so loud she could be heard throughout the office. Kristin was flabbergasted, stressed, and angry. She felt unjustly treated—especially since she was doing the agency a favor—and in any case, felt she didn't deserve to be tongue-lashed in front of her peers.

Knowing that she was too upset to make sense, Kristin focused all of her energy into calming down by breathing slowly and deeply and trying to relax her tense shoulders and jaw. Once she felt calm enough to move, she turned and left, telling Barbara, "We'll talk in the morning. I'm late for my tennis game." But after leaving the office, she was still trembling. The subsequent tennis game—hitting those balls—was exactly what she needed to become completely calm.

Later that evening, thinking about what she wanted to say to Barbara, Kristin reminded herself about how much Barbara had done for her and how much she liked and respected her . . . before *the incident*. The next morning she walked into Barbara's office calm, centered, and certain that the thing to do was confront her supervisor. She couldn't ignore what had happened, even though the job meant a lot to her, and she knew that having a chip on her shoulder would interfere with her work, which would be unacceptable. She looked Barbara in the eyes and calmly, but firmly, told her the reason she had been in the office dressed in a tennis dress. She also told her that being yelled at made her feel shamed and humiliated. "Maybe I shouldn't have come to the office wearing a tennis dress, but I truly thought I was helping, and in any event, yelling at me in front of everyone would never be helpful." It felt good for Kristin to get her feelings out. She had no idea how Barbara would react but was pleased when she apologized, promising never to yell at her again. And while Barbara did publicly yell at others every now and then, she never again yelled at Kristin, and they continued to work well together.

## How Well Do You Currently Manage Your Stress?

To assess your present ability to manage stress, ask yourself the following questions:

- ◈ When I feel agitated, do I know how to quickly calm myself?
- ◈ Can I easily let go of my anger?

◆ Can I turn to others at work to help me calm down and feel better?
◆ When I come home at night, do I walk in the door feeling alert and relaxed?
◆ Am I seldom distracted or moody?
◆ Am I able to recognize upsets that others seem to be experiencing?
◆ Do I easily turn to friends or family members for a calming influence?
◆ When my energy is low, do I know how to boost it?

If you answered yes to all of these questions, congratulations! You may be one of those rare people who can positively and quickly respond to stress in home and work relationships. If not, you are certainly not alone. In either case, the next chapter will guide you through a process to help you find the most helpful kinds of sensory input for you to become calm and focused so you can improve your relationships with more effective emotionally intelligent communications.

Mutual accord is mirrored in the facial and body gestures.

Top photo ©
iStockphoto.com/
Andrea Gingerich;
bottom photo
© 123RF/JY Lee.

The "just right" pressure of touch gives profound comfort.

Photo © iStockphoto.com/pidjoe.

Tender touch expresses shared affection.

Photo © iStockphoto.com/Ann Braga.

Opportunities
for playful
interaction are
everywhere!

Top photo ©
iStockphoto.com/
Diego Servo;
bottom photo
© Steven Barston.

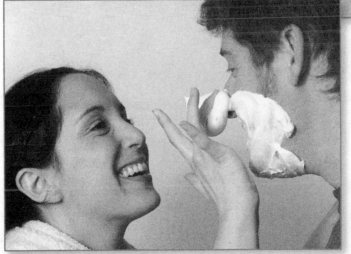

# 4 | Stress Busting

Our capacity to regulate our own stress is the *elastic* that provides us with a feeling of safety, giving us the ability to be emotionally available and engaged with other people, as well as to resolve relationship difficulties by returning communications to relaxed, energized states of awareness. Stress often compromises this ability. In the last chapter, we learned how to recognize stress; in this chapter, we find out exactly what we can do about it. Managing stress is an important prerequisite for us to experience our own emotions, as well as to tolerate the strong feelings of other people. Emotional intelligence is grounded in the emotions we feel and convey through nonverbal communications.

Without effectively and appropriately communicating emotions, there can be no truthful connection in relationships. By finding the ideal means of stress relief, you will be able to rapidly regain self-composure so that your actions will back up your words. You can learn to find the most effective methods for reducing your own stress or the stress of important people in your life by becoming a "stress-busting detective."

## Becoming a Stress-Busting Detective Helps Cope with Stress

Using elasticity to become a stress-busting detective can help you reduce your stress level by rapidly bringing you back into a state of equilibrium. No time here for a long, soothing bath or meditation. A stress-busting detective is one who seeks out the right kind of sensory input to soothe, comfort, and invigorate *in the moment.*

Being a stress-busting detective helps you take actions that calm and focus you at home and at work. This chapter on elasticity helps you explore a variety of sensory possibilities for bringing your nervous system back into balance. You can learn to create sensory-rich environments everywhere—in your car, in your office, or wherever you spend time. The exercises should be enjoyable and may improve your health and well-being, as well as your relationships.

Because each person's nervous system and overactive or underactive stress response patterns respond differently to sensory input, what works for you does not necessarily work for someone else. For example, certain kinds of music may relax one person but irritate another. The smell of incense can lift one person's distress, but another person may benefit most from candlelight.

Depending on a person's stress triggers, one person may need to slow down, another to speed up. Knowing the right kind of sensory input is essential to:

- **speed up**, if you are a person who is spaced out or depressed
- **slow down**, if you are a person who is angry or agitated
- **help get unstuck**, if you are a person who is frozen with anxiety

## Two Basic Approaches to Stress Busting

In the context of a relationship, stress needs to be managed quickly—in the moment—and composure restored before something is said or done that will be regretted. In that sense, it is elastic: there is a great deal of room for push and pull. Successful communication requires that we do something in a hurry to calm or energize ourselves, and then focus.

Once we become stressed, two basic types of rapid restorative measures can be used to return to a state of balance. Natural inclinations toward either social interactions or private and individual restorations may determine which general approach is more effective for a particular person:

- **Approaches that rely on interacting with others:** You can restore inner balance by seeking out someone who is calm, focused, and makes you feel safe. Being with a relaxed and alert friend, neighbor, colleague, or loved one can help you reorient yourself.
- **Approaches that engage your senses:** You can rapidly reverse the effects of stress by exposing yourself to sensory input that brings you back into balance. Sensory input encompasses what we hear, feel, touch, taste, and see.

## What Is a Stress-Busting Detective?

A detective attempts to unlock a mystery by looking for clues, testing the elasticity of a situation, gathering information, and putting it all together to make sense of what is learned. Here the mystery is, "How do different kinds of sensory input affect my nervous system?" The clues involve these senses:

- Movement (proprioceptive sense)
- Sight (visual sense)
- Touch (tactile sense)
- Sound (auditory sense)
- Smell (olfactory sense)
- Taste (gustatory sense)

Use the exercises that follow to help you explore a wide array of sensory possibilities. Explore at your own pace; take the time to enjoy yourself. Begin with the sensory experiences that appeal most, and take it from there. During your journey, look for sensory stimulants that:

◇ **both relax and energize you** and, at the same time, help you feel flexible, at ease, safe, and alert
◇ **have immediate impacts**, bringing about instantaneous and positive responses
◇ **are enjoyable**, bringing a smile to your face and warmth in your heart
◇ **are dependable**, consistently helping you feel more in control
◇ **are available**, are at hand or readily accessible

Here are several exercises to help you discover what works best for you. Try them in any order you wish—ideally, when you are not concerned about being interrupted.

## Movement (Proprioceptive Sense)

Get moving and get comfortable in your own space. Engage muscles and tendons:

◇ Stomp your feet—connect with the earth.
◇ Run around the room or even just in place.
◇ Jump up and down.
◇ Stretch out tense muscles, anytime, anywhere. For example, arch your neck and back, if you can.
◇ Dance around: invent new steps or repeat old ones.
◇ Roll your head: circle your head around in one direction, then the other.
◇ Tap your head lightly about with your fingertips.

- Give yourself a hand, foot, or head massage.
- Squeeze a rubbery stress ball or piece of play dough or clay.

## Sight (Visual Sense)

Surround yourself with images that make you feel sublime. Your imagination sometimes works just as well as actually seeing with your eyes:

- Nurture through nature: focusing on greenery can have a calming and lifting effect.
- Decorate with photos of loved ones or soothing scenes from nature.
- Adorn the walls with beautiful, funny, and delightful posters.
- Cut out pictures from magazines that make you laugh and feel good.
- Create small altars, and decorate them with mementos you find in nature.
- Surround yourself with colors that are delightful. For example, paint your walls with a hue that lifts your spirits.
- Close your eyes and picture a place or experience that brings a sense of calm and peacefulness.

## Touch (Tactile Sense)

Play with tactual sensations that relax and renew you:

- Wear materials that feel soft and comforting next to your body. For example, try silk, 100 percent cotton, or other smooth and light fabrics.

- Indulge your need to feel cooler or warmer: if it's hot, keep a cooling spray handy; if you are chilly, wrap something warm around your neck.
- Lightly stroke your face and arms.
- Wash your face with cool or warm water.
- Hold a comforting object such as a stuffed animal, a smooth rock, or a chenille scarf.

### Sound (Auditory Sense)

Experiment to discover sounds that you find renewing, supportive, and sustaining:

- Listen to nature's call—water, forest, wind, or bird sounds.
- Find a lift in gospel, religious, or spiritual music.
- Experiment with vocal sounds; sing or hum anything from grand opera to country twang.
- Lend an ear to instrumental music—orchestras, ensembles, and solos.
- Notice what sounds uplift and energize you. Save them in a format that you can listen to with earphones (e.g., iPod, CD, audiotape).

### Smell (Olfactory Sense)

Surround yourself with scents that calm and energize you. Some common calming and energizing aromas include: lavender, mint, orange, chamomile, rose, jasmine, eucalyptus, sage, basil, rosemary, and ginger. Soothing, invigorating scents come in a variety of natural, nonirritating forms:

- Buy or make potpourri from dried flowers, herbs, and leaves.
- Pick or buy fresh flowers such as roses, lilies, magnolias, and gardenias, which give off intense aromas.
- Enjoy the delicious fragrance of ripe fruit such as fresh strawberries.
- Permeate the air with essential oils applied to cotton, gauze, or a warmed lightbulb.

### Taste (Gustatory Sense)

Experiment with food *in moderation*. Food will work, but it's not the ideal comfort choice for people who have a weight problem or eating disorder. However, when it's an *appropriate* choice, mindfulness when eating may increase pleasure and reduce stress, while also reducing hunger.

- Take a small piece of something sweet (i.e., dark chocolate or a juicy berry), and let it dissolve slowly in your mouth. Savor every bite.
- Mix three or four different kinds of grapes in a bowl. Close your eyes, pick one, and slowly taste it. Notice its skin, inner flesh, and seeds, if any. See if you can identify the different types of grape solely through taste.
- Prepare something with lots of colors, textures, scents, and flavors (e.g., pink salmon, a bright green broccoli floret, and garlic mashed potatoes). Appreciate the color, smell, visual appearance, and flavor of each—a feast for all of the senses. Eat slowly with awareness, noticing how the different foods feel and taste on various parts of your tongue.

◇ Try a variety of flavors, the spice of life: a salty tortilla chip, a golden raisin, a spicy slice of pepperoni, a small piece of cheese, a crunchy bite of green apple, a pickle spear. Pay close attention to the differences.

Once you identify the sensory experiences that work best to relax, focus, and energize you, make them an ongoing part of your life at home, at work, while commuting—anywhere you spend time, which is *everywhere*.

## What Else Can You Do to Rapidly Relieve Stress?

Looking for something quick and powerful? Try these approaches to rapidly restore inner balance:

◇ **Deep breathing** involves not only the lungs, but also the abdomen. When you breathe down to the very bottom of your lungs, they press against the diaphragm (i.e., the partition between your heart and lungs and most of your digestive organs), causing your stomach to pooch out. If your breathing is shallow, using only your chest muscles to push air in and out of the lungs, you're not using your full lung capacity and not gaining maximum stress relief.
◇ **Progressive muscle relaxation** allows you to become aware of muscle tension that you might not realize you have. Controlling, contracting, and relaxing muscles in your body achieves quick relief from stress. Here's how:

1. Loosen your clothing, remove your shoes if possible, and sit comfortably.
2. Tighten the muscles in your toes as much as possible. Hold for a count of ten. Relax and enjoy the sensation of release from the tension.
3. Flex the muscles in your feet. Hold for a count of ten. Relax.
4. Move slowly up through your body—legs, abdomen, back, neck, face—contracting and relaxing muscles as you go.

◇ **Call someone you feel a close connection with and who is calm and alert**—someone emotionally at ease, intellectually focused, and available to you. If someone in your life knows how to listen *without interrupting or giving advice*, unloading your worries while talking to that person can help you rapidly restore balance. Good friends are valuable assets.

### Selecting the Best Techniques in the Moment
Ask yourself the following questions:

◇ **Does the elastic need to be pulled taut or released? Does my need for balance call for energizing or relaxing?** To feel centered, flexible, and alert, do you need activities that help you rev up or those that help you wind down?
◇ **What time do I have available?** Do you have time for a walk or a little exercise, or do you have only a minute?
◇ **Am I very social, with many friends and associates, or more of a loner?** Do you have a large group

of people to lean on, or will you rebalance on your own?

◇ **Do I have time to care for a pet?** Being around a friendly, loving, and relaxed animal is as soothing as being around a friendly, loving, and relaxed friend—only more dependably so.

◇ **Can I make time to play?** Joyous, playful experience can chase away the pain. Many people find that humor and playful activities magically help them feel balanced.

◇ **Do I use sensory input to soothe and energize myself?** What you see, hear, smell, touch, taste, and experience through movement and body position can restore the harmonious feelings of safety and attention, signaling balance.

## Recognizing and Responding Effectively to Stress

You met Irene, Norm, Ben, Mary Alice, Terri, and Stephanie in the preceding chapter on stress. All of these people struggled in their relationships because they failed to recognize and balance their own stress levels. Let's assume that they have learned to identify their stress response pattern and techniques to bring themselves back into balance.

◇ Irene is aware that pressure in her new job has affected her sleep *and her disposition*. Recognizing that she is in no mood to listen to her husband,

Alex, when she gets home from work, she asks him to accompany her on a quiet walk before dinner. By the time they return home, Irene is able to listen to Alex.

◆ Norm has learned to recognize anger as his most predictable response to stress. When he starts to lose his temper over a trivial incident, he asks himself what is so upsetting. Doing this helps Norm frame the problem in his own mind, without blaming another person, and gives him a chance to take the time to talk about it with a sympathetic listener.

◆ Ben used to collapse on the couch after a day of overscheduling and multitasking. He knows that he can stay alert for several more hours if he works out for fifteen minutes when he gets home.

◆ Mary Alice has learned that when she gets angry she loses focus. When upsetting things happen, she relies on listening to an audiotape of soothing music to calm herself down.

◆ Terri has become alert to the fact that she tends to seriously space out when under stress. She makes sure to eat small snacks routinely during the day. These little food infusions help her stay focused and alert.

◆ Stephanie has learned to pay attention to the fact that she often feels tense. To counteract the tension and soothe herself, she keeps a bowl of fresh flowers and a rose-scented candle on her desk. Her coworkers often compliment her on the beautiful, fragrant display.

5 | # Emotional Communication

The *glue* that holds the communication process together is the emotional exchange triggered by primary biological emotions, which include anger, sadness, fear, joy, and disgust. These emotions, essential for communication that engages others, have often been numbed or distorted by misattuned early relationships, but they *can* and *must be* reclaimed and restored to attract and preserve relationships.

## Needing Emotional Intelligence to Be a Great Communicator

Infants are a bundle of emotions, intensely experiencing fear, anger, sadness, and joy within the first eight weeks of life. Emotion is the glue that binds each of us to our first relationship, laying the foundation for all verbal and nonverbal communication in future relationships. Being in tune with your emotions and their correlating physical feelings accomplishes the following:

- It allows you to navigate satisfying, meaningful relationships.
- It helps you understand other people.
- It enables you to understand yourself.
- It empowers your communication process.
- It makes you "heart smart"—emotionally intelligent.

## Signs of Needing Greater Emotional Awareness

Consider the emotional responses of the following individuals in their home and work relationships:

- Bernie is a kind, steady, and dependable man whose emotional flatness inspired others to give him the nickname "Mr. Spock." His mood remains at a plateau—nothing is too exciting; nothing is worth arguing about. None of his interactions contain any "glue" to emotionally connect people to him. He can occasionally express a little excitement about his work but not about his love relationship with his wife. It was a surprise to Bernie when his wife inevitably filed for divorce. His flatness has also hurt his ability to advance at work. His bosses just can't imagine him motivating others.

# Quiz
## *Assessing Your Emotional Intelligence*

Becoming aware of your emotional experiences and communicating them effectively builds emotionally intelligent communication. The following quiz helps you assess how comfortable you are with your intense emotions.

⬦ **Do you experience feelings that flow,** encountering one emotion after another as your experiences change from moment to moment?

⬦ **Do you feel your emotions in your body,** based on felt experience that derives from visceral sensations?

⬦ **Do you experience discrete feelings and emotions,** such as anger, sadness, fear, joy—each of which is evident in subtle facial expressions?

⬦ **Can you experience intense feelings** that are strong enough to capture both your attention and that of others?

⬦ **Do you pay attention to your emotions?** Do they factor into your decision making?

If any of these experiences are unfamiliar, your emotions may be turned down or turned off.

⬦ Lin works hard at being a good wife. Attractive, caring, and hardworking, she takes everything seriously and seldom complains or criticizes. But her lack of spontaneity, humor, and playfulness is taking a toll on

her marriage, with her husband contemplating romantic involvements with other women. Lin's serious-
ness also limits her popularity at work. Because none
of her interactions are playful or full of emotion, her
coworkers tend to forget that she is there.

◇ Bill is admired by his colleagues and friends for his
kindness and generosity. Only his family knows about
his extremely short fuse. After an unprovoked verbal
outburst, Bill is predictably apologetic. When people
tell Bill's wife how lucky she is to have such a wonderful husband, she bites her lip, aware of how she and
her children suffer in their relationships with him.

Like misfiring pistons, these people cannot connect
with the strong emotions—the glue—needed for com-
pelling communication. They do not experience visceral
emotions that:

◇ **flow throughout the day**, changing from sadness to
happiness, from anger to joy in proportion to the
given situation
◇ **inform themselves of deeply felt needs** related to
mental and physical health
◇ **positively attract and hold the interest of others**,
powerfully communicating personal and interpersonal needs

Setting aside uncomfortable feelings has exacted a
toll. To improve their work and home lives, Bernie, Lin,
and Bill need to get in touch with their emotions. Each
needs to recognize the difference between basic visceral
emotions and the emotional coping strategies they use to

avoid, minimize, or attempt to manage the feelings they learned to quell long ago.

## Infant Emotional Communication and Adult Emotional Intelligence

An infant depends completely on nonverbal emotional means to communicate and thus satisfy its needs. This nonverbal, nonintellectual sensory experience is the life-sustaining heart and soul of each person's first relationship, and it continues to play a vital role in all of a person's future relationships.

Verbal skills begin to surface after the second year of life, but this new means of communicating does not render nonverbal communication skills obsolete. To the contrary, the template for communication in all relationships remains emotionally based. Nonverbal communication continues to affect:

- **your trust in others**—your belief that others will respond to your needs
- **your sense of self**—which is brought into focus by dyadic emotional exchanges (with important people in your life)
- **your self-image**—your self-confidence bolstered by the ability to communicate emotional needs
- **your relation to the environment**—your belief that the world is supportive and friendly
- **your distinguishing of self from non-self**—which is brought into perspective by success with dyadic emotional communication

◆ **your empathy**—your ability to comprehend the emotional experiences of others
◆ **your moral development**—your recognition that other people's feelings matter, too

## Factors That Limit Emotionally Intelligent Communication

We are born with an innate capacity for emotional intelligence, and emotion continues to play a pivotal role in all of our relationships. Yet many people lose touch with some or all of their emotions. How do we go from *experiencing* sadness, anger, fear, and joy to living an emotionally barren existence? There are two main factors that contribute to this loss.

### Reluctance to Experience All Emotions

The first factor is a cultural view that emotion is problematic. For centuries, cultural and religious institutions have denigrated emotion. People have been encouraged to think rather than feel. Although this disregard for emotion is at odds with the newer scientific and clinical understanding of brain function, preference for thought over feeling continues to prevail as the cultural norm.

Twenty years ago, when lifelong employment with one company was still the norm, and psychology was not yet a common practice, a large Japanese company retained me to restore morale in one of its divisions. A group of thirty-five top-level managers—valued employees who had worked for the company for more than a dozen years each, on average—had undergone a demoralizing shock when their departments were downsized due to automation. In a culture where supervising more people added to your prestige, they had, *in their own eyes*, become less valuable to the company and thus *lost face*. Although their salaries were not diminished by the downsizing, their confidence was, along with their focus on their work.

The company's leaders, who saw the downsizing only as a cost-saving measure that had nothing to do with their respect or appreciation for the employees, decided to give psychology a try to boost their employees' sagging morale. One reason I was chosen for the job was because it was assumed the managers would be less competitive with me, as I was a woman. Another reason was because a company consultant was familiar with my book, *Living Beyond Fear*, which pointed out how the power of hidden emotions can stall intent.

Before I began, the distinguished president of this international company questioned me thoroughly about exactly what I intended to do with his employees and the results I expected to accomplish. Displays of emotion—especially in men—were severely frowned upon in the Japanese culture of the time. Yet he was correct in thinking that I was going to encourage his employees not only to become more aware of their emotions but to share their emotions with their coworkers. I explained that turning down and turning off strong emotions is a draining and exhausting process that diminishes our ability to focus clearly and act decisively. Only by recognizing and acknowledging the emotions triggered by the downsizing would his managers be able to recover their energy and focus.

For four days, with the aid of a Japanese interpreter, the group of thirty-five managers explored what they called "feeling awareness" and "feeling communication." Three days were spent bringing numbed emotions to the surface and becoming consciously aware of them. Many of the emotions they expressed were painful and difficult to share, but the benefits of this sharing were apparent in the extraordinary creativity that manifested during our evening sessions. After dinner, we engaged in creative projects of all sorts, and the outpouring was truly incredible. One night, as a group, we made murals that were really gorgeous and worthy of display. Another night our creative brainstorming resulted in a new design for a common part used by the company. Buoyed by these experiences, the men explored their emotions at a deeper and deeper level each day. We spent the entire fourth day on strategies for retaining what they had learned about the value of feelings in a culture that frowned on sharing feelings in the workplace.

I left Japan feeling that this had been the best workshop I ever conducted. In spite of the cultural taboos, company loyalty had inspired this group to take emotional risks I never imagined possible. This impression was borne out when, two years later, I received a telephone call from the Japanese consultant who had first contacted me. He wanted to share the results of a two-year study undertaken after the workshop ended. The gains made at the workshop had been sustained. All of the men continued to perform at the high levels expected of them. The original group of thirty-five managers set up small groups in each of their departments based on the model of the quality-control circles popular at the time. These circles met regularly to talk about how they *felt* about the work they were doing. In addition, the original group met every other month to talk about their work, their emotions, and their lives.

## Disrupted Early Relationships

The second factor that limits or interferes with emotionally intelligent communication is a disrupted or disconnected relationship early in life. Painful and confusing emotional communication in infancy and early childhood often leads us to substitute less offensive, more intellectual *secondary* emotions during our interactions in adult relationships. Many people attempt to control their emotions rather than experience them.

Primary emotions—fear, anger, sadness, and joy—may become thwarted by life experiences. As you mature, so does the ability to distance yourself from raw emotion—a desirable and sometimes necessary end for people whose emotional experiences are frightening, painful, or confusing. With the abilities to speak, plan, and organize comes intellectual control. But this control also provides you with the means to displace, distort, and stifle unwanted emotions that you might be experiencing. To cope with emotion that seems overwhelming, painful, or undesirable, you develop secondary emotional responses such as the following:

◇ **Distracting yourself** with obsessive thoughts and behaviors that elicit controllable emotions is one way of coping. You may fabricate an elaborate fantasy life

that distracts you from feeling frighteningly alone.
Or you may engage in distracting compulsive and
addictive behaviors.

◆ **Sticking with an emotion that is bearable and unwav-
ering** is also very common. Being consistently angry
or constantly clowning may seem emotionally
intense, but such feelings are typically out of sync
with reality. Someone who is always kidding around
may be covering up feelings of fear or insecurity.
Someone who is always angry or sarcastic may be
deeply hurting beneath a hostile façade.

◆ **Shutting down or shutting out intense emotions**
manifests as having a depressed or diminished
response to overwhelming feelings of isolation
or fear. Physical and sexual abuse can trigger an
extreme state of emotional dissociation. People with
overwhelming feelings of anger or sadness may cope
by numbing themselves emotionally.

The price you pay for such counterproductive secondary emotional responses includes the following:

◆ **Shutting down your response to positive emotional
experiences.** You cannot realistically avoid or elim-
inate experiences of anger or sadness without also
eliminating joy.

◆ **Having an unhealthy mind-set.** It takes an enormous
amount of energy to cut off authentic emotional
experiences, leaving you stressed and devoid of the
energy needed to live an authentic life.

◆ **Damaging your relationships with others.** Your compulsive or addictive behaviors, and your anger or

withdrawal, will ultimately create stress in your work and personal relationships, and you will become more isolated and empty.

◇ **Withdrawing from yourself and the world.** The further you move away from experiencing your emotions, the more distant you become from others, as well as from yourself. Primary emotions are your best means for successful social contact. They lift and energize you, and they inform you about your own needs and the needs of others.

## Hal: Anger Held Him Captive

Hal couldn't seem brighter, more handsome, or more charming. Everyone who knows him casually admires him, but those who know him well—those who live and work closely with him—have mixed feelings because he makes their lives miserable with his sudden angry outbursts. Anything that Hal finds distressing, anything unpleasant, confusing, sad, or frightening, triggers his sudden anger. Everyone around him walks on eggshells, as they wonder what will trigger his next explosion.

Hal's behavior is predictably stressful to others and may be equally stressful for him. Sometimes people like Hal experience all the physiological responses to anger— they *feel* very angry—but instead of exploding, they implode. These are the "if looks could kill" folks or the people whose tension you could cut with a knife. They are at particular risk for cardiovascular and other serious stress-related health problems. Often their feelings of fear or sadness are experienced as being shameful and are not allowed to surface. This limits Hal's emotional responses to anger in a broad range of emotional situations.

Sarah comes from a background where anger was an unacceptable emotion. Therefore, she responds to painful and frustrating situations by becoming hurt, sad, or depressed. No matter what happens to her or how frustrated she becomes, Sarah doesn't get mad—she's afraid that she will lose control if she allows herself and others to know how angry and frustrated she feels. Sarah may have a reputation as "always being a nice, polite person," but there are also serious health consequences as well as relationship problems associated with being only nice all the time!

Both Hal and Sarah are stuck repeating emotions that don't change, just as the Japanese managers were stuck. They were experiencing the emotion of fear. In a real sense, the managers were traumatized. They felt helpless and overwhelmed by the downsizing—an event that in their eyes changed their identities. Trauma is an experience shaped by the eyes of the beholder. What frightens and traumatizes one person does not necessarily have the same effect on another.

Hal and Sarah, like the Japanese managers, would greatly improve their abilities to communicate, the quality of their lives, and their relationships with themselves and others by being able to experience a full range of emotions, rather than a very limited range.

## Do You Need to Further Develop Your Emotional Intelligence?

Ask yourself the following questions:

◈ **Do I routinely experience a variety of emotions?** A variety includes anger, sadness, fear, and joy.

◈ **Do I recognize my emotional triggers?** This ability is also an important part of what makes becoming a stress buster work. First you have to *feel* that something has shifted uncomfortably in your body. You're more agitated, tense, more numb, and less focused.

◈ **Do I accept all of my feelings?** Do I allow myself to *feel* angry, sad, or fearful?

◈ **Do I use my emotions as part of my decision-making process?** For example, if I don't feel comfortable with a doctor, dentist, or attorney, will I consider finding another qualified professional that I like?

◈ **Do I feel comfortable when other people exhibit or express strong feelings?** Or am I "in my own head," contemplating, rather than experiencing, feelings and sensations most of the time?

If you answered a clear yes to all five of the preceding questions, you may decide to skip the next chapter, "Raising Your Emotional Intelligence." If your answer to any of these questions was no, you will find that the processes presented in the next chapter will help you rebuild your ability to experience and appropriately express your intense emotions.

# 6 Raising Your Emotional Intelligence

**M**any of us, especially those who have experienced some form of trauma early in life, are not adequately in touch with the emotional experience necessary to communicate fully. Trauma includes a failed attachment relationship—as far as the brain is concerned, it is as traumatic to be emotionally ignored as an infant as it is to be abused. Over the years, the overwhelming feelings of anger, sadness, fear, and joy we were born with have been stifled or suppressed.

This chapter helps you reclaim the tuned-out and turned-off feelings that limit self-knowledge, self-expression, and sensitivity to others. It introduces exercises that teach you the difference between feelings triggered by emotional memories and intelligent emotions that can ground you and help you identify your deepest needs and values. Using a process that has been successful for more than thirty years, you can rebuild your emotional awareness and expression. An extensive four-part exercise helps you experience, accept, and benefit from the intense emotions that are key to sustaining intimacy.

## Restoring Your Birthright to Emotional Intelligence

The journey back to emotional awareness and emotional intelligence begins with a question: "What kinds of sensory input instantly make me feel relaxed, safe, calm, and focused?" Knowing the answer is especially important for people who have had overwhelming emotional experiences as a child. Once we have a safety net in place and know how to make ourselves feel good quickly and dependably, we can begin to explore the emotions that seem disagreeable or even frightening. The key to coping with questionable emotions is knowing that we are in control of them, and not the other way around.

In the following exercise, you learn to toggle back and forth between feelings you like and dislike—controlling your emotional experience. Its purpose is to help you experience *real* feelings and learn that you can tolerate even the feelings that seem difficult, enabling you to eventually engage in your relationships in a genuine and authentic manner.

I call this exercise "Riding the Waves" to convey the feeling of staying on top of a strong energy—not stopping the energy, but flowing with it. When you can integrate your feelings (i.e., the energetic emotional force within you) into your conscious thoughts, your emotional resources become an enormous asset—they are only a liability when they are hidden.

## An Investment of Time and Energy

Some books and programs for enhancing and building emotional intelligence assume that a lack of emotional intelligence is due to our misunderstanding about the important role emotions play in our work and home lives. The assumption is that if we just recognize the significance of our emotions, we will be able to use them appropriately—it is a matter of choice. But that's not true!

The belief that by simply having a positive attitude we can change our behavior when we're under stress is misguided. Belief alone won't change the reflexive emotional part of the brain, which reacts infinitely faster than the thinking intentional part of the brain. Saying something is so and believing that it is so does not necessarily make it so when preexisting conditions influence the way our brains and our bodies react and respond. Most of us may have started out with an ability to be aware of our feelings and emotions and thus access these wonderful resources. But if during infancy we experienced our emotions as overwhelming, our bodies have created ways and means of numbing and avoiding at least some intense emotions, thus impacting and changing our nervous systems.

We can reverse these patterns, but not without effort that will again alter our nervous systems. We need to learn that as adults we can tolerate our intense feelings by ourselves. This also opens doors to recognizing and responding appropriately to other people's feelings. In so doing, new neural circuitry is created in our brains that brings about new behavior. We can become emotionally intelligent even if we are not already, but it takes some practice and effort.

## Preparation

There are two ways of proceeding: You can stop reading at the end of this chapter, focus on riding the waves, and learn to practice and integrate this process before moving on. Or you may want to finish reading this book to see where it takes you, and then return to this chapter to do the exercises with the energy and focused attention that can result in healing and restorative, life-altering change.

To prepare for this exercise, first take the following steps:

1. Create a realistic plan for how you will structure the quality time needed for this intensely private exploration. Practice entails at least twenty to thirty minutes, but no more than sixty, on an almost daily basis for one to three months. Embark on this exercise

with the intention to really change—not just with your understanding and awareness, but with your ability to respond differently and for the better in almost any situation you encounter. You might also want to review the section in the Introduction about how to prepare for change.

2. Learn to be a stress-buster detective—especially if you suspect you were traumatized as an infant or young child. To regulate emotions, infants depend on their caretakers' responses to them, but adults can regulate themselves through sensory means—sights, sounds, smells, tastes, tactile sensations, and movements that calm, soothe, or energize the nervous system. Our needs are as individual as we are, and it is our own responsibility to pinpoint what regulates our particular nervous system. (Refer back to Chapter 4 if you need to reinforce or rediscover your own particular sensory stress-busting techniques.)

3. Ensure that the exercise ends promptly. Set a timer, pick a time well before bedtime, and try to avoid falling asleep. After you have done the exercise for ten to twenty minutes, *stop* and resume your normal activities. Take note that experiencing feelings of distress, such as while doing the exercise, can be nipped in the bud and leave you with feelings of increased energy, productivity, and self-confidence.

4. Find someone with whom you can share your experience later. Engage a loved one, friend, relative, colleague, counselor, therapist, or partner to whom you will describe what happened after you have practiced the exercise. This person needs to care about you and your emotions, and be someone who won't interrupt, give advice, or ask too many questions. Talking

about your emotional experience *after you have completed the exercise* will integrate the new learning into your life.

## The Exercise

There are four parts to becoming emotionally aware and alert.

### Part 1: Set Out with a Safe Anchor

First, your comfort level and sense of security must be ensured before you engage in this exercise to help you become more emotionally intelligent. Use the techniques you discovered during your investigations as a stress-busting detective (in Chapter 4) to establish an environment of sensory support:

- Find a private corner or niche in the world that meets your sensory needs.
- Make sure your surroundings feel completely safe and comfortable.
- Bask for a bit in the sensual pleasure that this setting affords you.
- Take off your shoes, and loosen your clothing.
- Take the phone off the hook, and lock the door. Hang a Do Not Disturb sign, if necessary.
- Find a comfortable chair that supports your back, or lie down—that is, if you're sure you won't drift off to sleep.
- If you're a clock watcher, set a timer.
- Stretch out to get a head start on loosening muscular tension.

◆ Music can play an instrumental role, as it is emotionally evocative. For example, if you've uncovered sadness in one exercise session and want to learn more about that feeling, listen to music that makes you feel sad. Use music to evoke the emotion you want to explore.

◆ Don't smoke, drink alcohol, or eat during this process.

### Part 2: Reconnect with Strong Feelings—Moderately

Take the time to experience visceral and muscular sensations in your body for a minimum of two minutes—repeating several times, up to ten minutes.

◆ **Tense, tighten, and then release** each part of your body, working from your feet up to the top of your head, and back down. Focus on each body part as you squeeze for a count of five to seven seconds before releasing the tension. Focus on all the muscles, bones, and deep feeling sensations in your toes all the way up to your neck and face. Allow every part of your body to *feel* completely limp and relaxed after you have squeezed and released them.

◆ **Clear your mind** of all extraneous thoughts. Close your eyes and take several slow, deep breaths, releasing your thoughts each time you exhale. Make sure to exhale as much air as you inhaled. Put one hand on your chest and the other on your belly. Are both of your hands moving? If not, breathe in a little more fully and let go a little more completely. As you continue, allow your body to sink comfortably into the chair, bed, or floor. Try repeating the phrases "soft

belly" and "soft chest" as you breathe in and out, for
a deeper sensation. Ridding yourself of thoughts is
not an easy undertaking. In fact, more likely than
not unwanted thoughts will intermittently pop
back into your consciousness. When that happens,
focus on your breathing, and again try to let go of
those thoughts while exhaling—concentrate on your
breathing and feeling sensations in your body.

◇ **Ride the waves by choosing an emotional trigger**,
something that had an emotional effect on you, such
as a small hurt or mildly irritating experience (e.g.,
maybe someone was rude or cut in front of you).
What you choose can be either an emotional memory or a bearable feeling that you are experiencing in
the moment.

◇ **Slowly scan your entire body** to find the spot where
a feeling is most intense. Is it in your stomach, chest,
shoulders, or somewhere else? Focus all of your
attention on this one area and direct your breath
to its core. Experience the physical sensations that
occur while you continue to breathe deeply.

◇ **If you become seriously uncomfortable, redirect your
focus** to the sensory input that you have identified as
calming and balancing—those you explored earlier
in the stress-busting detective exercise. Indulge these
pleasant feelings until you feel safe and comfortable.
When you're ready, delve back into the uncomfortable feelings you were exploring.

◇ **Repeat this process as often as necessary** until your
allotted time is up.

◇ **Congratulate yourself!** Give yourself a congratula-
tory pat on the back, or raise your arms in the air
and say, "Yeah, I did it!"

Every time you practice the exercise, you should feel a little more in control of your feelings.

As you become comfortable experiencing moderately intense emotional memories or current emotions, you can focus on increasingly intense feelings or emotional memories.

### Part 3: Go Deeper—Reconnect to Intense Emotions Confidently

This part develops your ability to safely experience emotions such as anger, sadness, fear, or joy without worry of repercussions. Surprisingly, joy can oftentimes be the most difficult emotion to fully experience. You may want to skip this part initially, until you are confident that you can comfortably embrace less-intense emotions while doing the first two parts of this exercise. When you are ready to embark on Part 3:

◆ Follow all the steps in the preceding Parts 1 and 2—but this time, select a memory with greater emotional intensity or stay with your feelings longer—for an *additional* ten to twenty minutes—tracking your emotional experience throughout the exercise. (Tracking for more than thirty minutes is unnecessary and can be unproductive.)

  Remember, if you become seriously uncomfortable, redirect your focus to the sensory input that you have identified as calming and balancing. Indulge the pleasant feelings until you feel safe and comfortable. Then when you're ready, delve back into the uncomfortable feelings you were exploring.

  Again, music can trigger emotional recall and intensify physical experience, but music tends to be personal, so your selection would best suit the emotions you are exploring, including sadness, fear, anxiety, and joy. A demonstration of the powerful emotions music can evoke is the way it is used to intensify emotional drama in films. But keep in mind that although music can help intensify your emotions, for this exercise it is not useful to select music that evokes more emotion than you can counter through relaxing and soothing.

◇ **Allow the feelings in your body to take root** by continuing to breathe deeply into the area of greatest intensity. You are trying to bring a fuzzy feeling into focus. Some people experience only physical sensations and emotions. At other times, these sensations are accompanied by visual memories. Everyone's experience is unique to them.

○ Scan your body for physical sensations, but also permit yourself to be emotionally engaged—frightened, angry, or sad—if that's how you feel.

○ You may begin with one feeling, but find that soon it shifts into another feeling or that the source of the feeling moves from one location in your body to a different place. Follow the new feeling as long as it proves to be more intense than the last.

○ If you're not experiencing much feeling of any sort, focus on just that—what it feels like to feel nothing. Intensify your experience by repeating, "I allow the feeling," with each breath, as long as it doesn't become a mental demand.

○ You'll know your intellect has intruded if the feeling you're trying to focus on tends to diminish rather than intensify.

◈ **Hang in there. Stay with the most intense feeling for ten to twenty minutes,** or as long as you can. Remember, it is important to stop after thirty minutes—the lessons will be learned by then, and it is important to integrate your thoughts with your feelings. (This is *not* emotional release; it's emotional integration.)

◈ **Don't force the issue and push for a release;** a bit at a time is just as effective and less taxing. The point here is to *allow* rather than *force* the feelings to emerge. This process is about trusting your body to indicate how much it wants you to feel in this moment. You'll get better at it over time.

Some people cry during this part of the process—not necessarily due to sadness, but because they've been repressing feelings for so long that the release can be intense. But tears are not necessary for a release. Some people moan or make other sounds, sometimes stretching or spontaneously moving their bodies during the process.

Trembling is common and a natural part of releasing and rebalancing after a traumatic experience—your mind may be saying an intense feeling is not OK. Just remind yourself that it *is* OK. So if you begin to tremble, continue to breathe deeply and hold your focus.

Again, if you become seriously uncomfortable, redirect your focus to sensory input that you know will calm, relax, and balance you. Remain with these pleasant feelings until you feel safe and comfortable. Then go back again to the uncomfortable feelings you were exploring.

Recording yourself stating the preceding steps and guidelines onto an audiocassette or computer file—maybe with some music in the background—can help you do the exercise without having to refer to notes.

### Part 4: Finish Strong—Seamlessly Switch Back to the World Around You

This final aspect of the exercise is integral to ending the process on the right note, empowering you with a greater sense of mastery and control. *Skipping this ending is not advised.*

◆ **When the time you've set aside for the exercise is over, rise and shine—get up, open your eyes wide, and stretch.** Stamp your feet, move your body, walk around, and wash your face if you've shed tears.

  If you have been crying hard, you might be tempted to continue on releasing emotional energy beyond the allotted time for the exercise. *Don't do it.* Redirect your focus, and go back to your life in the world. You've plunged into your feelings so you can reemerge, not remain.

◆ **Stop focusing exclusively on your feelings**, and redirect your thoughts toward your normal daily activities.

  Although your focus has now shifted from your inner world back to your outer life, you will retain some of the feeling awareness you just experienced.

◆ **Allow the feeling sensations to remain with you,** even though you aren't focusing on them.

◆ **Take stock of your energy and newfound clarity—** notice whether colors seem brighter, if sounds seem clearer. Are you accomplishing more than usual? You may feel more self-aware and more self-assured.

⬦ **Congratulate yourself.** This is not an easy exercise to do well—it takes courage and determination. But the benefits are well worth your efforts.

⬦ **Don't forget to describe this experience to someone who is a good listener**—someone who doesn't interrupt, interpret, or make comments about what you are telling him or her—within a few hours or a few days. Reinforce what you are learning. This is important for integration and an easy step to skip if you don't tend to talk to others about yourself.

Practice the exercise every day or as often as you can, until you can experience raw emotion without becoming overwhelmed. If after numerous attempts you remain frightened when performing the exercise, it might be advisable to seek the assistance of a mental health professional—someone with special training and expertise in trauma issues.

## Assessing Your Progress

Like building muscles in a gym, the more you flex emotions, the more "emotional muscle" you build. You wouldn't expect to be a bodybuilder after just five minutes. The more consistently you practice, the greater the change you'll experience in what you feel, think, and do. How will you know when you have practiced enough? In general you should feel more energy, experience more positive feelings (as well as other feelings),

# Raising Your Emotional Intelligence
*A Brief Guide*

## Setting the Stage

- Acquaint yourself with the kinds of sensory input that calm and soothe you.
- Create a private safe space with sensory materials that appeal to you.
- Make yourself comfortable, but take precautions so you don't fall asleep.
- Note the time you begin, so you will end promptly.

## The Exercise: Riding the Waves

- Tense and relax your body.
- Focus on breathing deeply enough to inflate both your belly and chest.
- The addition of music can intensify the experience.
- Begin with a less-intense experience, real feeling, or emotional memory.
- As your comfort level with the process increases, bring on more intense feelings or memories.
- You can also focus on the experience of nothing.
- End the exercise promptly when the twenty to thirty minutes are up.

## Ending Successfully

- At the conclusion of your practice time, redirect your focus (your thoughts) to the activities that would normally preoccupy you.
- Permit the feeling you had been focusing on to stay with you—but only as background sensation (not something you think about).
- Within thirty-six hours, talk briefly or at length with someone about your experience with the practice.
- Congratulate yourself.

and have a greater ability to concentrate your attention. You should feel more alive! More specifically, ask yourself the following:

- **Are you becoming more tolerant of experiencing intense feelings**, which include anger, sadness, fear, disgust, and joy?
- **Can you experience your emotions more and more as physical sensations**—in your stomach, chest, shoulders, and so on?
- **Do your feelings flow more freely during the day?** Are there times when you're happy and playful, and others when you're sad or mad? Do you find yourself feeling frightened, rather than mad, if someone cuts in front of your car?
- **Are you better able to experience your intense feelings**, or do you automatically try to numb them? Do you rationalize your feelings, altering them into more acceptable emotions?
- **Are you gaining an ability to calm down when you feel overwhelmed?**
- **Do you use emotional feedback more often in your decision-making processes?** When something sounds good but feels bad, do you give it a second thought?
- **Are you more able to comfortably talk about your emotions?**
- **Do your emotions help you better communicate?**

If you answered yes to most of these questions—congratulations! You have succeeded in raising your emotional intelligence.

# 7 Nonverbal Communication

The best verbal communication skills are not enough to create and sustain successful relationships. Good relationships, both at home and at work, require the ability to effectively communicate with emotional intelligence. Nonverbal communication is the *pulley* that attracts and holds the attention of others. It's the cornerstone of the language of emotional intelligence.

The attachment bond has shown that the language of infancy, which is emotionally laden and nonverbal, is such a powerful form of communication that it is responsible for shaping our mental, physical, and emotional development. Even after children learn to use words, nonverbal communication remains the basis of all relationships because the brain retains its tremendous receptivity to emotional cues throughout life. When you can effectively communicate in this special language, you will be able to maintain relationships that are more rewarding and productive.

The *pulley* of emotionally intelligent nonverbal communication is applied in the following ways:

- **Eye contact** is the visual sense that is dominant for most people and therefore is especially important in nonverbal communication. Visual contact may be soft, kindly, and warm, or hard, critical, and dismissive.
- **Facial expression** is composed by the face muscles, which indicate caring interest, concern, or understanding, or disinterest, anger, loathing, or contempt. Studies confirm that there are universal facial expressions that signify anger, fear, sadness, joy, and disgust.
- **Tone of voice** is moment-to-moment emotional expression conveyed by the sound of the voice. It may be warm, tender, or agreeable, or harsh, angry, or fearful.
- **Posture and gesture** are evidenced by someone's body being stiff, leaning backward, and immobile; or relaxed, leaning toward the other, arms open. The overall effect feels safe and inviting, or rejecting and threatening.
- **Touch** is the amount of pressure applied when you are in contact with someone via your fingers, such as when you grip someone's hand or exchange a hug. What "feels good" is relative and may be different

with each encounter; some people prefer strong pressure, others light pressure.

◆ **Intensity** reflects the amount of energy you project and the degree of force expressed in such cues as eye contact or tone of voice. Preferences vary among individuals and cultures.

◆ **Timing and pace** refer to the period between receiving and sending nonverbal communications and the swiftness of the communication process. The pace can dramatically impact the tone of emotional intelligence. Success is measured by the balance between your own preferences and what feels good to the other person.

◆ **Sounds that convey awareness and understanding** include sighs and sounds such as "hmmm" or "ahaaa." More than words, these sounds are the language of interest, understanding, compassion, and emotional intelligence.

## Nonverbal Communication Speaks Louder than Words

It takes more than words to create and secure productive, exciting, safe, and fulfilling relationships. Effectively maneuvering the pulley by accurately receiving and sending nonverbal cues can hold the attention of others, but too often we send signals we don't intend to convey. When this happens, both connection and trust can be lost in our relationships.

Ted, Arlene, and Jack are all verbally articulate, but they say one thing with words and another thing with their nonverbal communications. They don't pay attention to the delicate tug of the pulley—often with unfortunate results in their relationships:

◇ Ted thinks he has found the perfect love relationship when he meets Sharon, but she isn't so sure. Ted is very eligible: he is good-looking, hardworking, and a smooth talker. The trouble is, Ted doesn't seem to understand the difference between talking to himself and communicating with Sharon. When she has something to say, he replies before she can even finish her thought. This makes Sharon feel ignored. Ted loses out at work for the same reason. His inability to listen to others makes him unpopular with many of the people he most admires.

◇ Arlene is attractive and has no problem meeting eligible men—it's keeping them that's the problem! Even though she is funny and a good conversationalist who laughs and smiles constantly, she radiates tension. Arlene's shoulders and eyebrows are noticeably raised, her voice is shrill, and her body is stiff to touch. Being around Arlene makes many people feel uncomfortable. Arlene's job is in sales, and although she has a lot going for her, the discomfort she evokes in others undercuts her skills.

◇ Jack gets along with his colleagues at work, but not with those who matter most to him. If you were to ask them why, they would say that Jack is too intense. Rather than look at you, he devours you with his eyes. If he reaches out to take your hand, he lunges at it and then squeezes so hard that it hurts. Jack is a caring guy, but he has never learned how to be in sync with people. This awkwardness also limits his ability to advance to a managerial level at work. He just isn't seen as being good with others.

All of these articulate, well-intended people struggle in their attempts to connect with others. *None* of them are aware of the hidden messages they communicate.

Nonverbal communication is emotionally driven communication that answers the questions "Are you listening?" and "Do you understand and care?" We express the answers to these questions in the ways we talk, listen, look, move, and react—the way we pull and release on a pulley. These elements produce a sense of interest, trust, excitement, and desire for connection—or they generate fear, confusion, distrust, and disinterest.

## Setting the Stage for Successful Nonverbal Communication

Using the pulley of nonverbal communication with another person is a rapidly flowing interactive process that can be sensed only when we are alert and relaxed. Self-awareness and an understanding of the cues you may be sending are paired with the cues others send and pick up from you. To do this effectively, it is necessary to clear your mind of all distractions. If you are planning, analyzing, creating, fantasizing, talking to yourself, thinking about the other person or what to say, or thinking about anything other than your nonverbal communication with the other person, then you won't be paying attention to the moment-to-moment experience, have the presence of mind to pick up on nonverbal cues, or fully understand what's really going on in the conversation.

What you need to focus on, instead of thinking about anything, is what you momentarily hear, feel, sense, see, smell, and taste, as well as the reactions of the other person. This process enables you to pick up on important nonverbal signals such as the following:

⬥ "I don't understand" or "I don't fully understand," as evidenced by subtle changes in the expressive lines around the eyes and mouth and perhaps the entire head leaning slightly to one side. Most people have a difficult time admitting confusion or insufficient understanding, but it can be picked up in their nonverbal cues.

⬥ "What you are communicating is upsetting me," as evidenced by the subtle way the shoulders have hunched up, a look in the eyes, and a rise in voice pitch.

⬥ "I love being here with you," as evidenced by the congruency between a smile on the lips and an expression in the eyes, as well as the slight (or not so slight) lean forward.

⬥ "Something is wrong here!" as evidenced when the words you hear don't correspond to the nonverbal cues you are receiving; your emotional intelligence is at work!

There are times when you may want or need to plan out what you have to say. That's fine, but avoid doing the planning during the conversation if your goal is to sustain a felt connection with the other person. If you need to stop and think about something that has come up during a conversation before you proceed, you will interrupt the immediate nonverbal flow. But if you let the other person know that you feel this is necessary, that person may agree to a time-out or to pick up the conversation later. You could say:

◆ "Hmm, I need a moment to think."
◆ "This strikes me as appealing, but I also have reservations or concerns because . . ."
◆ "Can you give me a minute before we continue our discussion?"
◆ "I need to give this some thought before I answer. Can we discuss this later?"

When someone thinks out loud—such as talking about what he or she is thinking—it can be enlightening to be just a witness, if there is time. This can help the other person understand what is going on and feel included in the communication process, rather than excluded.

## How Stress Interferes with Nonverbal Communication

As we saw in Chapter 3, stress challenges your ability to be emotionally aware and to successfully communicate nonverbally. When you are agitated, withdrawn, or frightened, you look, hear, touch, and react differently than when you feel "just right." Also, one person's stress can block the communication process until both people again feel safe and can focus on one another. The following may happen when you are overcome by stress:

◇ **Old knee-jerk patterns of behavior take the place of newly learned patterns.** You may become absorbed in old thinking patterns and internal dialogue, freeze, or space out.

◇ **It is difficult to accurately convey your true feelings.** Although it is usually untrue, others tend to perceive you as angry or afraid of them.

◇ **It is more difficult to successfully understand emotionally intelligent communication.** You tend to be distracted from the reassuring messages or cues others may be sending you.

◇ **The capacity to influence or accurately read others is impaired.** You are more likely to make "bad" rather than "good" impressions on others.

◇ **Your upset easily triggers upset in others.** Upset is very contagious.

The best thing about recognizing when you are stressed is that it gives you the option to do something about it. Let's look at five people who have learned to recognize that they are stressed, and as a result, they have been able to manipulate their pulley to restore their state of equilibrium and communicate more successfully.

◇ Kim is feeling overwhelmed by new responsibilities that he has just been given at work. Although he is flattered to be offered this opportunity, he can't get his mind around the tasks at hand. Fortunately, his good buddy Frank is there for him to talk with. As he tells Frank what has happened, Kim notices that his jaw, shoulders, and chest relax. With his stress

reduced, he realizes that he really is capable and
competent for his new tasks.

◇ Carol narrowly avoided an accident on her way
home. Now her hands shake as she dresses for her
big date with Rob. Not wanting to spoil the romantic ambiance, she decides not to mention the near
miss. But Carol is so tense that when Rob hugs her,
she involuntarily flinches. She sees the hurt in his
eyes and realizes that she really can't hide her upset.
After calming herself with several deep breaths, she
looks into Rob's eyes and tells him what happened.
Relieved to know that he's not the problem, Rob
smiles and hugs her reassuringly.

◇ Kevin has had an extremely stressful workday where
anything that could go wrong did. All he wants to do
is go to bed, but before leaving for work that morning his wife told him that she had something important to discuss with him that evening. Recognizing
that his body feels too tense and exhausted for him
to be much of a listener, Kevin stops at the gym
before heading home. After a half-hour swim, his
energy is restored and he meets his wife with a broad
smile and a sincere look of interest.

◇ Nancy is so nervous about taking her qualifying
exams at work that she can't think clearly. All the
coffee she drank has made her nervous, jittery, and
unable to focus. Because Nancy knows that physical
exercise relaxes her mind and body, she puts on the
tennis shoes she keeps in her desk drawer and goes
for a run. Afterward she feels focused and ready for
the exam.

◆ Frank is attending his first office party with his fiancée, Vivian. Overwhelmed because he can't remember the names of many of the people, Frank fails to introduce Vivian. She feels hurt and becomes upset, but doesn't want to lose her temper. So she excuses herself and takes a little walk to calm down. During that time, she realizes Frank's dilemma. When she returns, Vivian gently takes Frank's arm. As they encounter new people, she introduces herself to them with a smile. Feeling reassured and more relaxed, Frank touches her hand in acknowledgment and can now remember many of the names, allowing him to introduce Vivian.

## Being Emotionally Aware Improves Nonverbal Communication

As we saw in Chapter 5, emotional recognition and expression are the *glue* that creates and maintains connection in relationships. Awareness of, comfort with, and respect for your own emotions makes you much more sensitive to other people's feelings as well. Being emotionally savvy gives you the ability to do the following:

◆ **Accurately read the emotional cues others send:** pick up on worry, sadness, grief, or stress.
◆ **Respond with nonverbal cues that reflect emotional intelligence, understanding, and care:** indicate that you notice and care.
◆ **Be congruent:** avoid confusing and confounding others with words that contradict your true feelings.

◆ **Know whether the relationship is meeting your own
    emotional needs:** give yourself a chance to repair the
    relationship or to move on.

Keep in mind that the emotional awareness you
uncovered in the previous chapter will greatly aid you
in sending and receiving nonverbal cues. Your ability to
understand, to effectively respond to the nonverbal cues
of others, and to send wordless cues yourself depends
on your emotional awareness and intelligence. Emotion
drives the cues and gives them their power to affect others. As you become more attuned to the sending and
receiving of nonverbal cues, your emotional awareness
will grow as well.

The awareness that comes from recognizing your
true feelings and the nonverbal signals that you send
others can be illuminating. Your eyes can be opened to
unknown parts of yourself that you didn't know existed
and aid you in transforming negative habits of mind.

## Using Nonverbal Communication
## to Manage and Avoid Conflict

Savvy nonverbal emotional communication is an
extremely important resource for managing and avoiding conflict. It begins with the ability to calm and soothe
ourselves and pick up on our moment-to-moment emotional experience—the moment-by-moment push and
pull of the pulley. This also allows us to pick up on the
emotional cues others are sending us and to react in ways
that are helpful rather than hurtful to the relationship.

Here are a few examples of nonverbal communication's power to defuse difficulties in relationships:

- Elaine is a drama queen. She is such a good actress that she often fools herself and others. Fortunately, however, her emotional fireworks do not fool her husband. When she runs amuck, he asks himself, "Do I really feel her upset in my body?" If the answer is no, he trusts that reaction because he also trusts his goodwill toward Elaine. He knows that criticizing her behavior will escalate the situation, so he comically pretends to get hysterical himself. Almost immediately, Elaine calms down and begins giggling. Elaine's emotionally intelligent boss also is not fooled or bullied by her antics and uses humor to de-escalate any uncomfortable situations.
- Rosario's husband is withdrawn and depressed about the loss of his job. Her heart breaks for him and she wants to help, but she knows that giving pity or advice isn't helpful. Instead, Rosario initiates long walks together where she doesn't say much but encourages her husband to talk about his feelings. During those walks, she takes his hand now and then and smiles reassuringly into his eyes. Within a couple of weeks, her husband has started to act like his old self and begins going to job interviews.
- Hal is in business with his son, Roy, and needs to talk to him about a problem Roy is creating. Even though Hal knows that Roy can become angry when criticized, Hal feels the situation can't be ignored any longer. When he finally sits down to have a discussion with his

son, Hal doesn't let Roy's defensiveness intimidate him. As Hal speaks his mind, he connects to the positive emotions he feels for his son. Because there is nothing critical or disrespectful in Hal's nonverbal communication, Roy stays cool and listens with interest.

Because Hal, Rosario, and Elaine's husband and boss have all learned to communicate with emotional intelligence and be attuned to the nonverbal cues of others, as well as their own nonverbal communication, they are able to defuse difficult situations and successfully manage and avoid conflict.

## Using Nonverbal Cues to Patch Up Communication Mistakes

No one is perfect—we all make mistakes all the time in relationships—but with emotionally savvy nonverbal communication, we can repair the damage.

Suppose that Ted, Arlene, and Jack (whom we met earlier in this chapter) learned to become more aware of the effects they inadvertently had on others? In addition to being more self-aware, they become attuned to the dance involved in sending and receiving wordless messages that are helpful in their relationships—even when they have "bad" days.

Notice what happens when they fall back into old patterns on especially stressful days but quickly become aware of the situation and make appropriate adjustments.

◆ Ted notices that Sharon's tone of voice has lost its warmth and realizes that he doesn't remember the last thing she said—he hasn't been listening to her! Looking chagrined and smiling apologetically, Ted leans forward, pulls the rope on his pulley, takes her hand, and looks directly into her eyes. She gives him a smile that says, "You're forgiven," along with a questioning look that he picks up on and answers in an emotionally engaging manner. Also, Ted's new ability to notice and accurately interpret the feelings of his coworkers has given his career an upward boost.

◆ Arlene notices that her date is tapping his fingers and that she has been swinging her leg and foot. He looks bored, and she feels tense all over. Taking a long, deep breath and a swallow of wine, she feels her shoulders drop and her jaw relax. Arlene leans across the table, releases the hold on her pulley, and breaks into a warm and radiant smile. Her date smiles back, and their eyes meet and hold. She has also used her new observational skills at work and is now much more comfortable interacting with others in that setting.

◆ Jack notices that his date seems to be leaning back and looks uncomfortable. Seeing her discomfort, he moves back in his seat, softens his gaze, puts his hands in his lap, and concentrates on following her lead. This change of behavior in Jack positively affects each of them. Jack's date rejiggers the force on her pulley by easing her guard; seeing her soften makes Jack feel more relaxed and confident. Jack, to his advantage, has also learned to notice and respond to the nonverbal cues of others at work, making him feel more confident and greatly improving his interactions with colleagues.

The powerful give-and-take of emotionally intelligent communication never ceases to flow, though its impact is often missed. The first step in acquiring greater awareness of our silent communication is to become impartial observers of ourselves and others. The following exercise facilitates this process and prepares you to take full advantage of what you'll learn in the next chapter.

## Taking a Good Look at What Might Be Difficult to See

Before we can ever hope to change our behavior, we have to fully recognize it. We need to see what we are doing, or what someone else is doing, in a clear light that isn't dimmed by criticism, judgment, blame, or shame. Negative self-talk isolates us from learning or changing our behavior. So if you catch yourself indulging in any sort of negative thought as you do the following exercise, stop! Keep trying, however, until you can observe yourself and others without placing a value on what you see. Bringing a sense of humor to the process of observation helps lighten and reframe it. (You will learn more about this in the chapters on humor and play.)

For the next week or so, carry a notebook with you wherever you go and jot down your observations of yourself, casual acquaintances—such as clerks, waiters, or parking attendants—and the people who are important to you, paying special attention to the glue of nonverbal communication. Of course you can't actually see yourself without the aid of a mirror or camera, but you can feel what is happening in your body as you look at someone and speak to or touch them. Also keep in mind that it is easier to track nonverbal communication during the pauses between words.

Observe, ask yourself, and note the following:

- ◆ **Eye contact:** Is this source of connection missing, too intense, or just right in yourself or in the person you are looking at?
- ◆ **Facial expression:** What is your face showing? Is it masklike and unexpressive, or emotionally present and filled with interest? What do you see as you look into the faces of others?
- ◆ **Tone of voice:** Does your voice project warmth, confidence, and delight, or is it strained and blocked? What do you hear as you listen to other people?
- ◆ **Posture and gesture:** Does your body feel still and immobile, or relaxed? Sensing the degree of tension in your shoulders and jaw answers this question. What do you observe about the degree of tension or relaxation in the body of the person you are speaking to?
- ◆ **Touch:** Remember, what feels good is relative. How do you like to be touched? Who do you like to have touching you? Is the difference between what you like and what the other person likes obvious to you?
- ◆ **Intensity:** Do you or the person you are communicating with seem flat, cool, and disinterested, or over-the-top and melodramatic? Again, this has as

much to do with what feels good to the other person as it does with what you personally prefer.

◆ **Timing and pace:** What happens when you or someone you care about makes an important statement? Does a response—not necessarily verbal—come too quickly or too slowly? Is there an easy flow of information back and forth?

◆ **Sounds that convey understanding:** Do you use sounds to indicate that you are attending to the other person? Do you pick up on sounds from others that indicate their caring or concern for you?

Because the point of this exercise is simply to observe, there are no right or wrong answers, only useful information that you will take to the next chapter.

You have seen how the ability to manage stress and to be emotionally aware enables you to sense the emotional cues others are sending and to respond appropriately. Next you will learn how to turn this knowledge into practice, a process that can change how people view you and how you view yourself.

# Speaking Louder Without Words than with Them

The preceding chapter introduced you to how nonverbal cues convey emotions more powerfully than words. The impact and forcefulness of nonverbal cues originate in the fact that they were our lifelines to survival as infants. The expressions on the faces we first saw; the tone, intensity, timing, and pace of the sounds we first heard; and the quality of touch we first felt created a nonverbal form of communication that is the mother language of all human life. Remove the give-and-take of these cues from our infancy, and we are likely to die. Nothing, either then or now, is better designed to grab and hold the attention of a person's nervous system than these wordless forms of communication.

In our fast-paced, goal-driven lives, it's easy to disconnect from the physical feelings and emotions that enable us to communicate nonverbally—especially if they didn't play a positive part in our early life experience. As we saw in the preceding chapter, when we are caught up in our heads thinking about something, it is very difficult to pick up and send the emotional cues that constitute nonverbal communication. Moreover, when our inner life is solely intellectual and we don't pause to attend to emotional communication, we may experience a loss of purpose and meaning, as the following story exemplifies.

## Frank: The Doctor Who Learned That He Had More to Offer than Just Medical Skill

Frank graduated at the top of his class from one of the most prestigious medical schools in the country. Intent on creating the best medical practice for cancer treatment, he brought together a distinguished group of specialists dedicated to saving lives through an aggressive assault on the disease. Frank did this when chemotherapy and radiation were still in their infancy, over twenty-five years ago. Single-minded and confident of his skills as a physician, he took it as a personal failure (though he knew better) when patients nonetheless died. After only twelve years—as many years as he had spent in training—and despite the fact that his practice had become the most popular oncology office connected to a major metropolitan hospital, Frank was ready to walk away from medicine. Then he met Sybil.

By the time Sybil's cancer was diagnosed, it had spread throughout her body and there was little hope for her recovery. Frank saw her several times in the office before she needed to be hospitalized. During the holidays, Frank's visits to patients in the hospital were always quick. Vital signs would be checked, he would ask patients if they were comfortable, and he might order pain medication before hurrying on. On Christmas Eve the hospital was empty, the staff greatly reduced, and the corridors quiet. Nonetheless, Frank was in his usual hurry. But before he could dash out of Sybil's room, she asked him why he was in such a rush to leave. Dumbstruck by her question, Frank turned around and blinked. Sybil continued, "I have the distinct impression that you can't bear the fact that I am dying." Shocked by her statement, all Frank could do was stare at Sybil and mutely nod. Thus began the closest friendship Frank had ever known.

He asked Sybil why she had no visitors and was alone at a time like this. She told him, "It's OK. I've sent my daughter and husband away because they get on my nerves. I think they probably love me, but their heads are so full of relentless chatter that they can't make space between the words to pay attention to me." Intrigued, Frank sat in a chair by Sybil's bedside and asked what she needed from him. "I want to you to stay with me while I die."

"I don't know that I know how to do that," Frank blurted out. "I'll teach you," she said. And so she did.

During the next ten days, Frank spent as much time as he could with Sybil before she died, and he learned to communicate in an entirely new way. Frank was the student and Sybil the teacher as he learned what it was like to truly *be* with another person. At first his typical rushed entry into her room was met by her request that he sit down and take a few deep breaths. "And how are *you* feeling?" she would gently ask. While Sybil patiently waited, Frank calmed down and focused on his feelings, comforted by her soft eyes and the warm smile that lit up her face. The way they communicated was a revelation to Frank. Sometimes they didn't talk at all, especially near the end. Frank just sat and held Sybil's hand while they looked at one another. The pleasure this silent time gave Frank was surprisingly intense and seemed mutual. Although Sybil was old enough to be his mother, what he felt for her seemed like love.

When Sybil died, Frank felt very sad but also renewed. His practice of medicine took on new meaning and purpose as a result of his relationship with her. Frank learned that a person's trust and respect is measured by not only what we do for them but how we *are* with them.

Nonverbal communication that expresses understanding and concern is a pulley that creates trust and draws others to us. These silent messages make others feel safe and inspire trust. No matter what we do for others, if we fail to take the time to stop and really see and be with them, our connection will be superficial.

## Opportunities That Nonverbal Cues Give

Our capacity to demonstrate emotional understanding and emotional intelligence depends on our ability to be attuned to nonverbal cues. Because these cues occur so rapidly and on a moment-to-moment basis, it is easy to miss their importance—especially when our focus is elsewhere. Like a dance with many complex movements that can be seen only in slow motion with the aid of a camera, nonverbal communication can appear complicated. If we think about it too much or try too hard, it will elude us; but if we are able to relax, secure in the understanding that our brains are already programmed for this kind of communication, it will come to us instinctively. Making a relaxed effort to be aware of nonverbal signals and use them improves our relationships and changes our lives by helping us:

◇ build relationships that give life meaning and purpose
◇ read the emotions that other people are experiencing
◇ better understand the emotional messages we send others
◇ create trust and emotional transparency in relationships
◇ resolve some problems without having to solve them

In the exercise at the end of Chapter 7, you observed the role that sending and receiving nonverbal cues plays in your life. The next section presents another exercise that will begin teaching your brain how to communicate nonverbally and pull the attention of others toward you.

## Observation Is the Beginning of New Learning

Careful observation is the oldest and best means we have of social learning. We learn many of our habits when we are young, but they can be relearned with observation and practice.

Take yourself out to have coffee or a meal, and choose a seat off to the side in clear view of the other customers. Do your best to be discreet; nobody likes to be stared at, and if people see you are looking at them, they may feel inhibited. Pay particular attention to facial expressions, eye contact, posture, gesture, touch, intensity, and timing and pace between people as they interact. If they are seated nearby, you might also pick up on sounds and tone of voice. Ask yourself the following:

◆ Is there a give-and-take to the communication you are observing?
◆ Do the couples who exhibit a positive exchange of nonverbal communication seem to be enjoying themselves the most?
◆ Do you see couples exchanging negative, dismissive, disinterested cues—perhaps couples that permit cell phones to continually interrupt their conversations?
◆ How does watching these interactions make you feel?
◆ Are some couples so invested in each other that their movements mirror one another's?

The more you observe the cues that bring other people together or keep them apart, the more aware you will become of the role that nonverbal communication plays in your own relationships. The more you practice using positive cues to build your relationships, the greater success you will have.

Recent studies and technology support the observations that we are profoundly and continually influenced by the nonverbal cues others send us. Nonverbal, emo-

tionally intelligent communication has such a powerful and lasting influence on the brain that it continues
to exert a profound influence even when words have
completely lost their meaning, as the following story
exemplifies.

## Linda, Who Communicates with People Who Have Lost Their Words

Frustrated by the inadequate care she found in most
board and care facilities, Linda put her life savings into
a small house in Venice, California, and opened a board
and care facility for women with dementia. Her training
as a physical therapist made Linda aware of the brain's
continued receptivity to sensual and emotional stimu-
lation in spite of damage to the thinking centers of the
brain. This awareness profoundly affected the way the
facility was designed and run.

As a visitor in this home for women who have all
but forgotten the names of those they most love, you
are struck by the liveliness of the people and the place.
Memory and the senses are stimulated by vivid colors;
everywhere you see photographs of loved ones and of
patients celebrating birthdays and holidays with the staff.
Occupants are physically active stirring cookie batter,
drying dishes, watering flowers in the garden, having
their nails painted, or walking with an attendant.

Although the women rarely say anything comprehen-
sible, caretakers find ways to communicate with them
through eye contact, laughter, touch, and with words of
encouragement spoken in loving and respectful tones. To

capture the attention of those they are trying to engage, caretakers may need to speak more loudly and move in closer to the residents. Those comfortable with physical contact are touched and massaged. Attendants watch for any signs of unhappiness or discomfort and usually are able to quickly address any problem that arises.

In this environment, which is rich in nonverbal communication and attentive to wordless signals, residents thrive—often living well into their nineties and even beyond. Today there is a program in place for medical residents to visit this little house and observe a standard of care that enables people with dementia to lead safe and happy lives. Wordless communication demonstrates its power to shape relationships in many settings—including some you would never expect.

## To Lead Well, We May Need to Follow

Linda found a means of creating a very positive environment in spite of severe limitations. One less obvious thing Linda does is to teach her staff to follow the resident's leads in nonverbal communication. If a resident reaches out, a game of high five can ensue; if a resident smiles and snuggles closer, that behavior is mirrored. When the staff want to create feelings of security, especially in young, insecure, or frail individuals, they mirror the person's nonverbal communication. Doing so creates a sense of trust and security and ensures that the staff stay within the resident's comfort zone.

In addition to encouraging some people to lead the way nonverbally, it is also wise to observe their preference for intensity. To be engaged, Linda's residents needed high-intensity communication. People differ in their needs and preferences for intensity. In the chapters on balancing stress, you learned that not everyone's brain and nervous system works as yours does. For example, someone who has a very active nervous system and who thinks fast will need to slow his or her pace and intensity to communicate well with colleagues or others whose nervous systems move at a slower pace.

In addition, there are cultural preferences for the delivery of nonverbal communication. Some cultural norms for both verbal and nonverbal communication are faster and more intense than others. Some invite touch, others avoid it. The awareness of these differences is especially important in the global business world.

To fully connect with some people, we need to intensify our eye contact, voice, or pace. At other times, we have to slow our pace, distance ourselves, or lower our tone to create safety and comfort in the relationship. If the best possible relationship is our goal, we are wise to make accommodations. Again, take note of the following as you go about improving your relationships:

◆ Where or when do you observe people operating at a faster or more intense pace than yours?
◆ Where or when do you observe people operating at a slower or less intense pace than yours?
◆ What do you do or not do to accommodate the differences you experience?

There are no right or wrong answers here. It all has to do with what you want from the relationship. But if what you want is more safety and a deeper connection, you need to move beyond observation and into action. The following story is about a group of creative people who used video recording technology to do just that.

## Bill, Who Learned to See Himself as Others Saw Him

Perhaps you observe disconnects during your interactions, but remain unsure of the role your nonverbal communication plays in creating the relationship rifts you experience.

One way of learning more about your delivery of nonverbal cues is to capture your communication process in action on video. This was Bill's intention when he became part of a group that met weekly to film one another.

The idea was to take turns behind and in front of the camera, and the purpose was for the group members to see themselves as others saw them. Most people came with friends who, like themselves, were experiencing relationship problems. Two or three individuals would communicate with their partners for half an hour or so in front of the camera. People who were not being taped watched silently or took a turn operating the camera. They were discouraged from discussing the contents of the tapes as a group. Such discussion was restricted to avoid sharing judgments and preconceptions with the person being taped, and thus affecting what they might discover while watching the tape later. Each person was given a copy of their own tape to view as many times as they liked at home during the week.

Participants were instructed to view their tapes by themselves at home, with the sound turned down, and they were advised to set aside judgments or criticisms of themselves while watching. Instead of thinking about what they saw, they were encouraged to focus on observing their own body language, facial expressions, pace, tone of voice, and degree of eye contact. In addition, they were encouraged to ask themselves:

- Am I overwhelming or underwhelming my partner?
- Am I speaking too forcefully or not forcefully enough?
- Am I giving my partner more information than he or she can absorb?
- Am I responding to my partner's nonverbal cues?
- Does my communication reflect interest and caring?

Bill joined the group thinking he was a good listener, as well as a caring, sensitive, and spiritual person. He had recently gone through a devastating divorce that left him feeling victimized and hopeless. Seeing himself on tape, with the sound muffled, was a revelation for him. On the screen he saw someone who appeared distant and uninvolved. During most of the segment, he sat with his arms and outstretched legs crossed and a cap pulled over his eyes—an impossible position in which to carefully view anyone or to make eye contact. He looked rather bored, although he actually hadn't been at the time. He also appeared to do the lion's share of the talking—plowing ahead without stopping to absorb the nonverbal cues that his partner was sending.

The tape revealed some less-than-flattering things to Bill about himself, but it also gave him a new perspective on why his relationships had always been so troublesome. The person he saw in the tape was not someone who reached out to others or even seemed interested in knowing them. Maybe he was more responsible for the bad things that happened to him than he realized. Maybe he wasn't a victim after all!

Bill ran and reran the tape until he not only saw his nonverbal process but also felt it in his body. He experienced the feelings that resulted from his movements away from others or his loss of eye contact. This later helped him recognize when he had fallen back or was about to fall back into old patterns of behavior. The process of changing was also supported by the ease with which he was now establishing new friendships and new relationships—at work, as well as in his social life. The experience of seeing himself on tape made such an impression on Bill that he continued to find opportunities to be recorded on film and to watch these recordings. He saved these tapes as reminders to himself of the ongoing possibilities for change and growth.

## Using Visual and Auditory Aids to Increase Communication Awareness

You can learn, as Bill did, to see yourself as others see you. The age of electronic and digital gadgets affords opportunities for us to see and hear ourselves as others do. This technique also can provide opportunities for you to gauge how well you experience and pick up on nonverbal cues that others send you.

The following devices capture you in real time. If you can slow down the visual devices when you watch them, viewing one frame at a time, you may see and hear even more. But whatever you capture, the process itself will make you more aware of sending and receiving nonverbal, emotionally intelligent communication—provided that you don't bring self-criticism into the task. Today a wealth of relatively inexpensive electronic gear can be used to capture images of yourself and your communication process. These include:

◇ **Video camera:** Using a tripod, frame your face and hands in the viewfinder to capture your facial expressions and body language. Start recording a conversation between you and your partner. When finished, you can watch your nonverbal communication as you listen to your verbal expression. Then rewind and replay it in slow motion to see even more. Your partner may want to trade places during the filming to see him- or herself in action. You also can set the video to record both of you at the same time. If you have access to a second camera, you can videotape both of you at the same time, with full-face impressions of each person.

◇ **Digital camera:** Ask someone to take a series of photos of you while you are engaged in conversation. You won't hear the words, but the images can be very revealing.

◇ **Audio recorder:** Capture the tone and resonance of your voice, and the timing and pace during a conversation. Listen most carefully to the sounds that are not words at all.

If you lack such technical devices, you can always assume the role of a "fly on the wall" and observe the nonverbal communication of others. In addition to looking at and listening to yourself, you can practice with others who also want to become more proficient nonverbal communicators. Ask them to give you feedback on what they observe about your nonverbal communication and interactions. Keep in mind that this is best approached in a spirit of fun and play with someone you trust to have your best interests, and their own, at heart, and not as an opportunity to express harsh criticism.

## Doing Nothing—*Very* Effectively

In some settings, nonverbal communication is particularly effective and gives us an edge. There are some settings where nonverbal communication can have profound influences on our relationships and on our well-being. The first of these has to do with problem solving and the second with assessing toxic environments. Problem solving is the one subject that radically differs in home and work settings when it comes to nonverbal communication. At work, we are usually expected to solve problems that require thoughtful solutions, but this is not the case in most of our other relationships. In these situations, we are called upon to use our skills in nonverbal, emotionally intelligent communication.

When people come to us with problems, often they are not asking us to solve them. Therefore, unless someone comes to us with a problem and specifically requests a solution, we are probably being asked to simply listen. Most people, young as well as old, want the satisfaction of solving their own problems. By listening, we contribute to this satisfaction and build trust in the relationship.

## Building Relationships by Helping Others Solve Problems

Friends and family members are usually asking us to care and listen when they bring us their problems. If we can give them what they want, we have an opportunity to make our relationships more rewarding. Unfortunately, many people miss such opportunities. Here is an exercise for creating a more in-depth relationship with someone who comes to you with a problem. It takes time to listen, so before you do the following, make sure that you want to listen and you have the time.

The next time a friend or family member comes to you with a problem, take a deep breath and before you jump in with advice, do the following:

◇ **Look into the other person's face and observe:** What level of concern is being expressed? How important is this problem to this person?

◇ **Look into the other person's eyes and observe:** What intensity of emotion do you see expressed in the person's eyes?

◇ **Listen to the other person's pacing and tone of voice and observe:** What do you notice about the volume, intensity, and timing of the person's voice?

◇ **Watch the other person's posture and gestures and observe:** How are you being affected by what is being conveyed?

◇ **Observe if or when the other person uses touch:** If so, how and when is touch employed?

◇ **Let the other person know that you are with them:** Use your face, eyes, and body to express your concern.

◆ **Stay connected:** Use sounds, rather than words, to indicate that you are with them and listening.

The point here is to say as little as possible yourself—at least the first few times you practice what may be a new way of responding to problems. Speak only if you don't understand what is being said and need to ask a question for clarification. Communication is always a give-and-take process, so some of what the other person communicates to you will be in response to what you are communicating to that person through cues in your face, body, and voice.

When we make the time and show an interest in helping loved ones solve their own problems, we are building relationships and being supportive. But not all relationships are supportive—some deplete, confuse, and exhaust us. When this is the case, it is to our advantage to be aware of how we are being affected so we can take action and make positive changes.

## Gauging the Effects of Hurtful Nonverbal Communication

Awareness of nonverbal cues gives us an opportunity to better assess the impact others may have on us. But in gauging our response, it is wise to also consider the effect that our own critical or judgmental thinking can exert. Before you ask yourself the following questions, consider how you may be contributing to your own negative experience. In addition, before beginning, take time to relieve your stress when you find yourself agitated, withdrawn, or frozen. Once you are relaxed, notice whether you con-

tinue to feel disturbed. If so, ask yourself the following
questions:

- What is going on in this environment that is disturbing me?
- What is this person doing that bothers me?
- Is someone sending nonverbal cues that make me feel
  uncomfortable?
- Are this person's nonverbal cues a response to something I am conveying?
- What are my options for moving to a more comfortable position within the environment or leaving it
  altogether if necessary?

The purpose of asking these questions is to help you
become more aware of the nonverbal, as well as verbal, cues that signal your discomfort. There are no right
or wrong answers, only opportunities for improving a
situation.

When we communicate without words, a broad new
world of possibilities for improving relationships opens
up to us. In this new more social world, mistakes are
permitted because they can be observed and corrected,
and we have a powerful means for drawing others to us.
Effective use of nonverbal communication, as well as
interactive play and humor (which will be discussed in
the following chapter), help us to overcome many challenging situations and to experience shared joy in all
types of relationships.

# 9 Playfulness and Humor

layfulness and humor, the naturally high *ladder*, enable us to navigate awkward, difficult, and embarrassing issues. Mutually shared positive experiences also lift us up, strengthen our resolve, help us find inner resources needed to cope with disappointment and heartbreak, and give us the incentive to sustain a positive connection with others at work and our loved ones at home.

All emotional sharing builds strong and lasting relationship bonds, but sharing humor and sheer delight adds a unique restorative and healing element, reducing stress and mending fences. Connecting in exciting and meaningful ways using the ladder of playful, humorous interactive communication keeps relationships creative, productive, pleasurable, and on track.

## Relying on Humor and Play to Reduce Stress and Mend Fences

Conflict and stress can undermine even the best verbal skills, but playful communication strengthens, repairs, and restores relationships. Not only is mutual play fun, it's an opportunity to relax, renew, and refresh yourself with others at home and at work. Play, the most joyous form of nonverbal communication, enables us to:

◇ **Take hardships in stride.** Laughter helps us view frustrations and disappointments from new perspectives; it enables us to survive hard times, setbacks, and frustrations.
◇ **Smoothe over differences.** We are able to say things that might be difficult without creating a flap.
◇ **Simultaneously relax and energize.** Play delights the nervous system, relieving fatigue and relaxing the body, allowing us to be more productive.
◇ **Become more creative.** Easing the need to control releases rigidity and inflexibility, inviting creativity to bubble up.
◇ **Experience mutual joy.** Nothing in life is more delicious than sharing joy with someone we love.

Adults also play to learn and to improve their health.

# Laughter and Play Eliminate Stress and Improve Relationships

Laughter and play fill you with joy. They are natural antidotes for whatever ails you, including stress, pain, and conflict. Nothing works faster or more dependably to alter stress and bring your body and mind back into balance. Climbing the ladder of laughter and fun does its good work on your nervous system rapidly and efficiently. Within a few seconds, a stressful situation can become an occasion for relaxed merriment.

With so much power to heal and renew, the ability to laugh easily and frequently is a tremendous resource for surmounting problems and hardships in relationships. Even the most stressful situations can be transformed, because laughter and play:

◆ keep you grounded, focused, alert, and attentive
◆ quickly and deeply relax your body, slowing heart rate and breathing and reducing blood pressure
◆ inspire hope—good feelings replace negative expectations with positive expectations
◆ trigger survival instincts

By protecting your nervous system and keeping you focused, laughter and play offer you opportunities to thrive even in inhospitable environments. Findings ways to create a playful environment in even the most dire situation can dramatically transform the outcome of your circumstances, as illustrated in the following section.

## Babies Thrive on Laughter and Play

The World Health Organization (WHO) recently undertook a series of studies that brought laughter and play into some of the bleakest settings on earth: in refugee camps, such as in Darfur, where people are jammed together for years in the smallest imaginable quarters with insufficient food, little water, and poor medical care. The aid workers who arrived to provide whatever food, water, and medical care they had also encouraged a group of mothers in the camp to create a playful environment for their infants. Bits of string, cotton, and paper picked up from the ground were used to transform the cubbyholes in which they lived into imaginative worlds of play. A similar group of mothers and infants in the same camp were just given food.

Remarkably, these WHO studies revealed that not only were mothers who played with their infants less likely to become depressed, but also their infants thrived. The infants who were played with, who laughed and smiled with their mothers, grew bigger and stronger than the infants whose mothers didn't engage in play. As we now know, this not only made their present circumstance a bit more bearable, but also set up healthy attachments for future relationships.

## Why Laughter and Play Are So Powerful

When you laugh and play, your body is calmed and energized by the release of natural opiates—endorphins that relax you physically and lift you up the ladder emotionally. These powerful chemicals, which are released by the brain, not only improve self-confidence and social skills, but they also override physical and emotional pain, anger, and disappointment and strengthen your immune system, boosting your body's defenses against disease.

It is now widely recognized that laughter reduces stress and promotes healing. Children and older patients in hospitals are encouraged to laugh and play with help from clowns or animals that come to visit them. And we know from the examples of orphanages in Rumania during the cold war that infant growth can be stunted by emotional neglect. An antidote to high levels of stress and a key to survival is laughter and play.

One of the most important factors linking laughter and play to survival is its social dimension. The women who avoided depression despite their quality of life in the refugee camps and the infants who grew without abundant food and shelter did so because they laughed and played together.

The immensely powerful impact that laughter, play, and humor can have is connected to experiences that include others. Shared joy impacts your brain and nervous system to a degree that laughing alone does not.

## The Importance of Play as a Shared Experience

Play is something we can do alone or as a spectator, but in relationships, play is always a shared experience—a source of pleasure made more joyous by the mutuality of the experience. We play together in relationships to:

- **Practice spontaneity:** we get out of our heads and away from our troubles.
- **Let go of defensiveness:** it helps us forget, briefly, our judgments, criticisms, and doubts.
- **Release inhibitions:** our fear of holding back and holding on are set aside.
- **Calm and energize:** our hearts and minds are stimulated and regulated.
- **Become emotionally authentic:** deeply felt emotion is allowed to rise to the surface.

But interactive play is not a competitive game; it has to be interesting and equally fun for both people. There can be no winners or losers. Something isn't funny unless it is funny to *both parties*—and this includes teasing. Each person has to be excited and drawn into the experience. When this is the case, nothing is more delightful.

However, if playfulness isn't mutually experienced, it may detract from rather than support a relationship, like a ladder without anything to lean on, as the following exemplify:

- Charlie, a fireman in Los Angeles, was fed dog food in his lunch of spaghetti and meatballs. Not only did he find the prank not humorous, he sued the city for one million dollars. His coworkers in the fire department believed they were just having fun with a colleague, but they didn't check out their assumptions first. Big mistake—Charlie won his suit with the city. Years of friendship and camaraderie have dissolved under the weight of litigation.

- Barbara's feet are perpetually cold when she gets into bed at night—even in warm weather—but she has what she thinks is a playful solution. Her "fun" idea is to warm her icy feet on her husband Jed's warm body—but this isn't a game he enjoys. Jed has repeatedly told Barbara that he doesn't appreciate being used as a foot warmer, but she just laughs at his complaints. Lately, Jed has taken to sleeping at the far end of the bed, a solution that creates distance between them as a couple; the ladder Barbara was trying to cross with humor and fun only opened up a deeper chasm.

- Fletcher and Phyllis are husband and wife professionals who work for the same literary agency. Fletcher enjoys teasing and has been known to get into Phyllis's files and leave little personal notes in projects she is working on. More than once Phyllis has emailed files containing messages from Fletcher that she didn't know were there. Fletcher finds this very amusing, but Phyllis is embarrassed and feels undermined.

Playfulness that strengthens relationships is a joint investment that can help us over many of life's small and large hurdles. However, even if a joke is meant to be positive, when it doesn't consider the other person's viewpoint, it can undermine trust and goodwill. Before jumping into jokes and humor, it is critical to consider your motives and the other person's frame of mind.

## Playfulness Helps Navigate Awkward and Embarrassing Issues

The ladder of play and humor often can help bridge a subject that may be embarrassing or awkward to friends and colleagues. In playful settings, we hear things differently and can tolerate learning things about ourselves that we otherwise might find unpleasant or even painful. Consider the following:

⬥ Francine got moved to a new cubicle at work near Anna, who people made fun of behind her back—holding their noses and avoiding her—because she exuded an unpleasant body odor. Francine decided to strike up a conversation with Anna and began chatting about holiday gifts she was given, including several bottles of cologne. Because Anna seemed interested, Francine brought various colognes to work, and the two women made a game of trying on a different scent each day and guessing its brand. While having fun and getting to know her coworker better, Anna's body odor ceased being a problem at work.

⬥ Maryann fell and broke her right wrist. She was in a cast past her elbow and felt totally clumsy and frustrated trying to use her left hand. At dinner, she struggled to get food onto her fork and into her mouth, often dropping it all over her lap. Her husband, Tom, quietly moved his own fork to his left hand to join her in the challenge, and for the next couple of weeks they both laughed as food landed on the floor.

⬥ Connie's husband came home from work sweaty and dirty. She was totally turned off by his odor and appearance and couldn't imagine being intimate with him under such circumstances. But when she suggested he should take a shower, he got angry and accused her of not appreciating his choice of jobs. Now, Connie turns on the water, begins playfully peeling off his clothes, and joins him in the shower.

⬥ Maria and Enrique have been trying to conceive for much longer than either expected. They are now undergoing fertility treatments, including pills she's taking and injections into her abdomen. Their sex life has been greatly disrupted, and they are beginning to snap at each other. To change direction and make a game out of their circumstances, they take turns being responsible for the injections and joke about the size of the needle compared to the size of "something else" that would have to be inserted in order to conceive.

All of these people have been able to find playful ways to navigate awkward and embarrassing issues. Be aware, however, that whenever you approach ego-sensitive subjects, you can be treading on thin ice. To be sure that you're not making a situation worse, ask yourself the following before playfully addressing what might be an ego-sensitive subject:

⬥ Are you feeling calm, energetic, and warmly connected to your partner or coworker?
⬥ Is it your true intention to communicate positive feelings?
⬥ Are you certain that your humorous gesture will be understood and appreciated?

- Are you aware of the emotional tone of the nonverbal messages you are sending?
- Are you sensitive to the nonverbal signals your partner or coworker is sending?
- Do you back off if your partner or colleague seems hurt or angry?
- If you say or do something that offends, is it easy for you to immediately apologize?

## How Humor Can Help Resolve Conflict

We all have our bad days when our nervous systems get overloaded and we do things that we regret—such as overreacting and sending out e-mails that have more to do with our state of mind than with the subject addressed. Nowadays it seems as though most people have very full plates and more things to do than they really have the time for; being overwhelmed is a common state of mind. Even people who have learned to recognize when they are feeling stressed and know what to do about it (e.g., go to the golf course or for a run, meditate, or ask for a foot rub) will do or say things they regret.

But people who can navigate with humor do not have to revert to shaming or blaming—themselves or others—when what they have done can be undone. Appropriately used humor enables you to face up to your actions and take responsibility without shame or blame.

Making fun of things people find frustrating has always been the mainstay of comedians. Lucille Ball, one of the most famous and beloved comediennes of all times, wove her career around the challenges of married love. Lucy satirized the petty jealousies and irritations couples feel toward one another and came up with playful, hilariously funny resolutions.

Assuming we have a solid basis for a friendly or loving relationship, making fun of things that cause us stress is something we can do often in relationships by:

◇ joking about our frustrations
◇ making a game out of pretending to like things we really dislike
◇ spoofing and playfully exaggerating problems
◇ making up playful games that help us get our points across

Play gives us an opportunity to turn frustrations and negative experiences into opportunities for shared fun and intimacy. In the context of mutual play, we replace judgment and criticism with humor, and we can say and do things that might be awkward or offensive in other contexts.

Here are several examples of ways that people have lightened up tension and dampened anger in relationships:

◇ Jamie, who is eight months pregnant with her first baby, is shopping for nursery wallpaper with her husband, Ted. They disagree about the pattern and are getting into a heated discussion in the middle of a crowded store. Realizing that emotions are escalating over a minor matter, Ted suddenly and loudly declares, "Clearly, we have irreconcilable differences. Want to get a divorce?" People in the store stare at them uncomfortably, and Jamie is momentarily stunned. Then she and Ted both burst into peals of laughter and go on to choose wallpaper.

- After retirement, Alex still goes up on the roof by means of an actual ladder to clean out the gutters. His wife, Angie, has told him numerous times that it scares her when he gets up there. Today, instead of her usual complaints, she yells up to him, "You know, it's husbands like you who turn wives into nags." Alex laughs and comes down from the roof.

- Shalene is a distracted driver. When her carpooling buddy, Kayla, is the passenger, she gets very agitated at Shalene's inattentiveness. One time, Shalene is oblivious to the light changing to green and is still sitting and musing when Kayla says, "So, girlfriend, what color *would* you like the light to be?"

- It is a tradition at John's company to honor the employee of the year with a "roast"—a dinner at which coworkers poke fun at the honoree. These roasts highlight the most obvious features that make this individual unique (like a caricature of Jay Leno's chin), while allowing others to let off a little steam about the things that may actually bother them about the person. In the end, though, each presenter offers sincere praise and appreciation for their honored colleague.

## Play Helps Us Survive Heartbreak and Loss

Play is a powerful survival mechanism that supports our ability to surmount life's hardships and tragedies. Entire civilizations that were brought to their knees have survived over time by enlisting the force of humor and play to counteract their distress. Intense emotions can change rapidly. One moment we can be in the throes of grief and the next laughing at a ridiculous memory or comment.

Humor and play are respites from sadness and pain, but more than just being a time-out, play also imbues us with the courage and strength to find new sources of meaning and hope. They are ladders that can point us in a new direction, such as in the following examples:

- Andy has had a hard life. He became an alcoholic as a teenager and struggled for years before overcoming his addiction. He has many regrets, including lost jobs, failed marriages, and children he abandoned emotionally. But his failures don't keep him from joking about his past with family and close friends. The jokes and kidding—poking fun at himself, not at others—prevent him from forgetting his problem with alcohol and help him integrate his past with the present.
- Tracy's life has also been difficult because of her insecurities and eating disorders. Today, healthier and happier, Tracy encourages intimacy and avoids secrecy or denial about her past by speaking openly about her regrets and mistakes. Her secret for putting people at ease with her painful disclosures is that she talks about them humorously. Her sense of humor allows her to be honest and open—but not self-pitying—with her family, friends, and coworkers, and this endears her to them.
- Teresa sits beside her husband's hospital bed, holding his wrinkled hand as she watches the machines monitor his pulse, oxygen intake, and heartbeat. After more than a half-century together, she gently says,

"You know you have to outlive me—I'm covered by your insurance." Len turns to her, and with the twinkle in his eye clearly visible even under these stressful circumstances, he replies, "Darling, why didn't you mention that sooner—I could have postponed this heart attack!"

◆ Sidney recently lost his job after thirty-one years of loyal service and is worried about finding another job at his age. The hurt of this loss is unlike anything he could have expected, but his playfulness and sense of humor keep him afloat. Sid's ability to laugh and joke about his "paid vacation" on unemployment bring him the motivation to go out and look for a new position, and the strength to present himself as the capable worker that he is.

## Laughter Provides a Way to Survive Intolerable Situations

This chapter wouldn't be complete without retelling a story that was made into the movie *Life Is Beautiful*. The story demonstrates how humor and playfulness empower our ability to support one another and stay connected to joy and to life in the face of a cruel and insane reality. An Italian Jewish man and his young son are imprisoned in a forced labor camp and subjected to years of brutality and deprivation. However, the devoted father uses playful fantasy to shield his little boy from the desperation of their lives. Everything that happens becomes an opportunity to create another playful fantasy. Soldiers are merely actors playing the parts of bad guys, and harsh realities are games to be played that invite fanciful solutions. In this way, the little boy is protected from the death and brutality that surrounds him. And in the end, the child survives unscathed.

Fortunately, most of us don't have to use humor and play to completely blot out our realities. But we, too, can benefit by softening the harder edges of reality with a coating of humor.

## Humor Helps to Avoid Depression

The WHO studies of the mothers in refugee camps, who avoided depression as their infants thrived on play and laughter, makes a point about the relationship between laughter and depression. Most depression is not clinical depression. Rather, it is the result of painful and disappointing experiences that mark us with shame, self-loathing, bitterness, helplessness, and hopelessness. Laughter and the ability to see things from a humorous perspective make us resilient and give us a means for fighting many types of depression.

Humor offsets depression by:

◇ **Putting things into perspective:** Most situations are not as bleak as they appear to be when looked at from a playful and humorous point of view.
◇ **Connecting us to others:** People are attracted to happy, funny individuals. Laughter and goodwill draw others to you and keep them by your side.
◇ **Providing opportunities for the release of endorphins:** Endorphins are the brain chemicals that over-

ride sadness and negative thoughts—laughter triggers the production of natural opiates that relax your body and lift your spirit.

Another example of how humor can offset depression can be found in biographies of Abraham Lincoln. Recognized by historians as a great man and visionary leader, nevertheless, Lincoln fought depression throughout his life. Tragedies during his youth were compounded by personal losses as an adult and his political struggles, which made him a very unpopular president until the end of the Civil War. But throughout, Lincoln's famous humor prevailed, as did he. Renowned for his ability to laugh at himself and cast a humorous eye on his defaulters, Abraham Lincoln remained thoughtful, focused, and attentive to his responsibilities and commitments, in spite of his well-documented depression.

## The Misuse of Humor

Playfulness helps us cope. Life at every age is full of major and minor challenges that humor and play can help us survive. But because joy is an emotion, there are times when humor may not be what it seems to be—when it becomes a cover for avoiding, rather than surviving, painful emotions.

The necessity for mutual enjoyment when we play together in relationships has already been discussed in this chapter. There are also other instances where playing isn't inclusive fun. Joy, like the other primary emotions of anger, sadness, and fear, can become a way to avoid less-acceptable emotions. Playfulness can be a disguise for hiding feelings of fear, hurt, anger, and disappointment that we don't want to feel or don't know how to express.

We can be funny about the truth—but covering up the truth isn't funny. When we use humor and playfulness as a cover for other emotions, we create confusion and mistrust in our relationships. The following are examples of misplaced humor:

- Sharon has a perpetual smile on her face and is always upbeat. Nothing ever seems to get her down. No matter what happens to her or to anyone else, she remains smiling and cheerful. Sharon's one-note personality is a tip-off that other less-playful emotions may lie beneath her perpetually sunny and playful persona. In reality, Sharon may be depressed and afraid to express darker feelings.
- In his relationship with Kevin, Philip is often jealous and possessive. He is suspicious of every conversation Kevin has with any other man. But Philip has never learned to openly discuss his insecurities and fears. Instead, he uses what he thinks is humor to express his feelings. However, his "jokes" usually have a biting, almost hostile edge and do not seem at all funny to Kevin, who responds with coldness and withdrawal.
- Stacy uses playfulness and wit to conceal her stress and fatigue. Unfortunately, she has become so good at concealment that she often fails to notice how

depleted she is—and keeps going long after she should stop to rest and recoup. Her hidden exhaustion limits her capacity to be productive at work or invest in a relationship.

For cues as to whether or not humor is being used to conceal other emotions, you can ask the following questions of yourself:

- Do nonverbal communication signals—such as tone of voice, intensity, timing—feel genuinely humorous to you, or do you experience them as forced or "not right" somehow?
- Is humor the only emotion you routinely express, or is there a mixture of other emotions that at least occasionally includes sadness, fear, and anger?

In addition to being the most delightful nonverbal communication skill, a sense of humor is powerful. Laughter and playfulness give life its zest. They also provide a means for you to transform fear and quiet desperation into communications that reflect hope, joy, and positive expectations. If you do not have a sense of humor, you are hardly alone. Humor is learned, and if you didn't learn it when you were young, you can learn it now. Chapter 10 can teach you how.

# 10 Joyful Practices to Strengthen Communication

Laughter is a birthright that gives you the boost needed to climb up and out of life's inevitable obstacles, disappointments, and losses. The part of the brain that connects to laughter is among the first components of the nervous system to come on line after birth. Infants begin smiling during the first weeks of life and laugh out loud within months of being born.

Some people do not retain the ability to laugh easily and often, because it wasn't part of their early life experience. But it's never too late to learn to develop and embrace joyful feelings, which are the keys to facing and overcoming the ups and downs of daily living. The capacity for generating fun and initiating interactive playfulness helps us manage stress and take negative emotions in stride. In addition to infusing your experiences with zest and fun, humor and play give you a leg up and over many challenges by helping you:

- put problems into perspective—they give you a means for standing back and getting a better view of a situation
- remove stress from frustrating situations
- be infused with powerful natural opiates, which energize your body and lift your spirits even when faced with challenging and unpleasant experiences
- think better, as well as feel better—humor and play energize thinking and inspire creative problem solving

Along with all of these extraordinary benefits, an added value of humor and playfulness is that they can be developed throughout life. Even if you did not acquire a sense of humor in childhood, you can now. You can also further develop your existing sense of humor. The more you do this, the more your ability to laugh will nurture you and your relationships.

As a starting point, let's begin with an assessment of how much time and attention you typically devote to laughter, play, and having fun on a day-to-day basis.

## Playing with Problems Transforms Them

Life dependably presents us with challenges that can either crush us or become playthings for our imaginations. When we "become the problem" and take ourselves too

# Quiz
## *How Much of Your Life Do You Devote to Laughter and Play?*

This exercise asks you to record positive experiences—
a process that is easily accomplished with the aid of an
inexpensive counting device. The little plastic recorder fits
in the palm of your hand, and you give it a gentle squeeze
to add another number. Of course, you can also use a
notebook to jot down your observations.

Each day during the next week, give yourself the
following points every time you:

- smile—1 point
- laugh out loud—2 points
- tell a joke—3 points
- play a game with someone—5 points
- watch or listen to a funny show or movie—10 points

After you have completed this exercise and have a total
score for each day and the entire week, ask yourself:

- Are you satisfied with your score or would you like to
  have collected more points?
- Did your score change significantly from day to day? Do
  you know why?
- Do you have more fun in or out of the office? Why did
  you answer as you did?
- If your score changed on the weekend, was it higher or
  lower? What accounts for the change?
- Do you know people who make you laugh? Do you
  make it a point to be with these people?
- Are there humorless parts of your life? If you answered
  yes, why do you think this is true?

The scores you compile and answers you give are less important than what they mean to you—there is no right or wrong number nor a scale indicating where you should fall. The more important questions are whether you are satisfied with the time and attention you give to feeling good, and if you think you could or should be having more fun.

If an infusion of joy into your life is a resource that you want to cultivate, read on. This chapter contains suggestions for bringing more humor and playfulness to your daily experiences and your communication processes.

seriously, we court shame and crushing feelings of unworthiness. But even shame is no match for the intensely good feelings that the cultivation of humor can provide. By fostering humor and playfulness, we can transform many of our problems into opportunities for creative learning.

Playing with problems seems to come naturally to children. When they are confused or afraid, they make their problems into a game, giving them a sense of control and an opportunity to experiment with solutions. People who are fortunate enough to have never stopped playing retain this creative ability. Those who have lost this problem-solving resource or never learned it at all can master or regain it by deliberately choosing to interact with others in playful ways.

### Roy, Who Learned That Play Could Be a Problem Solver

Roy was always interested in golf and looked forward to having more time to devote to the game. When he started playing seriously after his semiretirement, his love for the game began. He joined a golf club, bought a good set of clubs, took lessons, and became a reasonably good golfer.

But the more he invested, the less he enjoyed himself. Now that he knew how to play, it seemed he no longer had excuses for making mistakes! So even though he began a day of golf feeling great, by the end of the day he was in an angry mood. Every time he made a bad swing, Roy got so upset with himself that he lost his focus; from then on his game went downhill. He concluded that if he couldn't change the way he felt about himself when he made mistakes, golf would be the death of him.

Close to throwing in the towel, Roy realized that the friends he played with also affected his mood. When he played with people who focused more on having fun than on their scores, he was less critical of himself. So Roy asked Bill, the golfer he liked best, how he avoided becoming frustrated when he hit bad shots—as all golfers do. Bill's answer was, "I focus on the things I like about the game, instead of my mistakes. The sky doesn't fall down because you hit a bad shot—there will be other opportunities to hit good shots. What's the point of doing something you like, if you're not having fun?"

Roy took Bill's comments to heart and found that shifting his focus from "the glass half empty" to "the glass half full" made his golfing experience much more enjoyable. His score improved too, though he focused less on it. This was especially true when he played with people who didn't take the game, or themselves, too seriously.

Roy carried over into other parts of his life the realization that he had the power to add more fun to his life by shifting his focus from what didn't work to what felt good. In viewing problems more lightly, Roy did not dismiss responsibility for them, but gained energy to face them more constructively. He also used this lighter, more fun-loving perspective while working with clients in his part-time job as a consultant. Roy helped put other people's problems into a more balanced perspective by asking them the same questions he had been asked, "Is this really as serious a matter as you are making it?" Most of the time the answer was no, although occasionally a problem was real enough to warrant serious and immediate action.

Besides giving you a new perspective on problems and difficulties, playful communication also does the following:

- **Builds trust** between yourself and others, providing a base for creative problem solving
- **Gives you stress-free time-outs** that restore energy and focus
- **Relaxes defensiveness in others**, as it's hard to be oppositional with someone who makes you laugh

## Replacing Blame, Criticism, and Judgment with Humor and Playfulness

The following exercise can help you replace negative evaluations with humor and playfulness. It gives you an opportunity to put problems between yourself and others into perspective by making a *really* big deal out of your flaws and mistakes.

## The Sky Is Falling Down, but I'm
## Tired of Holding It Up

Ask yourself the following questions about a problem that you frequently beat yourself up for having:

- Is it worth getting upset over?
- Is it worth upsetting others?
- Is it that important?
- Is it that bad?
- Is it that irreparable?
- Is it really your problem?

If you answered yes to any of these questions, why aren't you taking action? Could it be that your energy is being exhausted by judgment, criticism, and blame, leaving you unable to take constructive action?

Here is an interesting way to reframe the preceding questions: ask yourself, "If I knew that I had only one year to live, how would I *now* answer those questions?" Have any or all of your answers changed? If the problem really is serious, do you now feel more motivated to do something about it?

Finally, use your imagination to answer the preceding questions from the perspective of an impartial observer looking at your life—someone who can see shades of gray, as well as black and white.

## Humor Lightens the Load

The skills of humor and play can be developed with practice, and the more you practice, the more possibilities you'll discover. In addition to helping you solve problems, these skills can also significantly reduce your workload.

Starting the day with laughter or taking time-outs during the day to laugh brings your nervous system into balance. Humor and play can calm and soothe away the stress of overly active, overly busy, and intense lives. The ability to remain focused and productive is strained by the frequent need to carry larger and larger workloads and work longer hours. Time-outs for pleasure and joy go a long way toward compensating for the added burden and the accompanying stress. Beginning the day on the right foot—a foot primed for laughter and pleasure—makes what you have to do feel easier.

## Setting the Stage for Working and Living Well with Laughter

Alice, a senior partner in a large, high-pressure law firm, starts the day early and ends it late. However, she does not begin workdays with case reviews; rather, she starts with a laugh fest. The partners in her firm sit around the conference table over coffee and bagels each morning, taking turns telling jokes and funny stories. Because laughter is very contagious, almost immediately everyone is laughing hysterically. This ritual is observed no matter what important or urgent business is pending. Although a new partner sometimes questions the need to begin each day with a meeting that is seemingly unrelated to work, before long that partner comes to understand the benefits.

Something magical happens to the group as it gives itself over to uproarious laughter—something that carries over into the day's work and into the relationships the partners share among themselves and with their clients.

As the day unfolds, brief moments of shared remembrance with accompanying chuckles keep the atmosphere light and pleasant, even though the work is intense.

Besides the enhancements in quality of the firm's work environment, there are also real cost-savings that stem from infrequent absenteeism and lowered medical insurance expenses. Morale is high, and the partners experience few conflicts that are not resolved quickly and easily. Most members of the group consider the early morning laugh fests the high point of their day and wouldn't miss them for the world.

## How Can You Experience the Contagious Nature of Laughter?

Here is an exercise for you to experience the contagious nature of laughter.

### The "I Am Absolutely Not Going to Laugh" Game

Laughter is contagious. When you are with a group of people who are laughing, it is almost impossible not to be swept away by laughter yourself. Test this premise by gathering together a group of people—they can be strangers, as well as friends.

- Take turns telling jokes or funny stories, or watch a funny show together, all the while trying your best not to laugh.
- Ask each person to predict how long he or she can hold out before laughing.
- Offer a prize of some sort to the individual who can resist laughing for the longest period of time.

This kind of game can also work wonders to lighten up minor disappointments. As the disappointing experience is elaborated on, participants remain absolutely serious—no one is allowed to so much as snicker.

## Play Pays Off in Creativity

Creativity is another bonus of playfulness. The goodwill and camaraderie that humor and play generate are of particular value in businesses that feed on constant change, such as the electronics industry. A prominent Internet company exemplifies this principle. Employees are encouraged to play like kids—which supports exceptional productivity in these working adults. Also, employees are encouraged to dress very casually and ride their scooters up and down the hallways.

Lunches are occasions for festive parties. Food in the corporate cafeteria is free, and so plentiful and imaginative that you would think it was designed by Willy Wonka. There are bins of colorful candies and gums, and food selections from junk to gourmet from all over the world. People are encouraged to eat together in the attractive dining room or on the huge ocean-view balcony peppered with brightly colored umbrella tables. People are encouraged to drop in whenever the mood strikes them for a handful of jelly berries or rock candy.

This workplace buzzes around the clock with a "keep the kids happy" atmosphere, which ultimately brings out the best in some of the most creative minds around.

## The "Making Something out of Nothing" Game

Toys are a relatively new concept. For most of the history of human evolution, children didn't have toys and instead played with whatever they could find that was lying around. Imagination flourished, while the brain was primed for survival.

In that spirit, here is an exercise inspired by a friend, Bernie DeKoven, author, teacher, and creator of whimsical games of all sorts, that gives you a chance to make up a game of play using junk objects that you find lying around.

This game can be played with two people, but more is preferable, because its purpose is to inspire teamwork and camaraderie, as well as fun and creativity. The game works as well with participants who don't know one another as it does with those who are familiar to each other. It's most fun when you have enough people to make competing teams—friendly competition adds extra zest to a game.

1. First decide on the game you want to make. Or do you want to make up a new game? Perhaps you want a ball game, a card game, or a game using marbles, stones, twigs, rubber bands, or chips of wood—or to create a game you are already familiar with using junk? You can play a checkers-like game with almost anything on hand that can be sorted out into two piles: for example, pieces of smooth glass, wood, or paper, half of which are marked in one color and half in another color.
2. Then investigate stuff that would be appropriate to play with—junk that is lying around and is not

important to anyone. Common objects such as old socks, old shoes, newspaper that can be crushed and balled up, and broom handles make great playthings. You could make sock puppets or use broom handles as bats or hockey sticks to use with balls made out of almost anything that can be packed tightly together or inside a sock or stocking. Next, work together as a team for a predetermined amount of time to construct your game.

3. Finally, with everyone participating, play the junk-yard game you have just created.

These same principles can be applied to board games, works of communal art, or fantasy designs for future products. They all demonstrate the hilarious joy of inter-active creativity and the fun of playing and working together.

## Play Is a Springboard for Renewal

Smart bosses looking to keep their bottom lines up delib-erately plan playful environments for their employees, but the value of playfulness is evident in other aspects of life as well. People who incorporate humor and play into their daily lives find that it renews them and all of their rela-tionships in many contexts, including some that come as a surprise.

One of the wonders of childhood is that there is no dis-tinction between work and play. The work of development, of becoming the best you can be, is inspired by creative play.

Those who have forgotten how to play can learn a great deal from little children who have, as yet, not forgotten.

## Jane: The Artist Who Learned from Children's Play

Jane was an artist who worked part-time at home making greeting cards. She lived with her husband in a large apartment complex. Across from Jane's apartment lived two bright little sisters—one was two, the other three. While their mother worked, their grandmother looked after them, but she watched television most of the time, so the girls busied themselves elsewhere. They loved to make paper dolls.

One day when Jane's door was open, the sisters noticed that her apartment was full of colorful pencils and paper. From then on, they made it a point to stand by expectantly whenever they saw Jane entering her apartment, until the day she invited them in. The girls told her about their interest in making paper dolls, and Jane asked the question they had been waiting to hear, "Would you like to make dolls and doll clothing with the boxes of brightly colored cloth and crayon bits that I have saved?" Overjoyed, the children showed up at Jane's apartment every day. At first Jane just helped as the girls cut out patterns and watched them play; but soon, at their urging, she joined them on the floor, laughing and pretending. Because she was an only child and had no sibling for a playmate, Jane was fascinated and drawn into the process. After joining in their play, she was hooked, spending hours a week for the next year drawing and playing with the children.

The year that Jane spent playing with the sisters, before they entered nursery school, was transformative for her. Not only did playing with them end her loneliness and mild boredom, it sparked her imagination. Her own artwork began to flourish, and she took up painting, something she hadn't done in years, with success. The greatest surprise, however, was the effect it had on her ten-year marriage. Over the years Jane's relationship with her husband had grown predictable—pleasant, but a little dull. Playing with the children rekindled the playfulness Jane had once brought to the relationship, and this brought out the playful side of her husband, as well, who told Jane, "You've turned into your old self, the person who I fell in love with."

## How Can You Add Fun and Playfulness to Your Life?

The more things that you do to develop a sense of humor, the more humorous you will become.

Many people did not experience mutual play as infants and don't know how to play with others just for the fun of it. The good news is this is something you can learn! The more you play, the easier it is to play, and the more you practice, the more you learn. A commitment to play begins by putting aside other things to have quality time for playing on a regular basis. If you feel self-conscious and concerned about how you'll look and sound to others, which often is a big factor that limits a person's playfulness, remember that as a baby you were just naturally playful— you did not worry about the reactions of other people.

How you learn to play depends on your preferences. You can do the following:

◈ Loosen up your funny bones by watching funny movies and sitcoms.

◈ Take an improvisation comedy class. Make this into an exercise; practice makes you better.

◈ Volunteer to play the Easter Bunny or Santa Claus for a family gathering, a party with coworkers, or a social function for an organization.

◈ Throw a costume party. Dressing up and pretending is a good way to get into playfulness.

◈ Begin by observing what you already do that borders on fun:
  ○ Jokes?
  ○ Movies?
  ○ Eating?
  ○ Making faces in the mirror when you're alone?
  ○ Dressing up or down?
  ○ Daydreaming?

Unless you also learn to play for fun with other people, you won't hone the joyous skills you need to make your relationships flourish. One of the best ways to learn something new is to practice with "experts." Here are some additional things you can do to immerse yourself in mutual play:

◈ **Play with animals.** Puppies, kittens, and young animals in general are eager playmates and ever ready to be playfully engaged. Make playdates with friends' pets or get your own.

◈ **Play with babies and young children.** The real authorities in human play are children, especially young children. Playing with children who know you and trust you is a wonderful way to learn from the experts.

◇ **Play with customer service people.** Most people in the service industry are very social; many are playful, and they often welcome playful banter. You find them in places such as checkout stands, restaurants, and reservation counters.

As humor and play become an integrated part of your life, your creativity will flourish and new discoveries for playing with friends, coworkers, acquaintances, and loved ones will occur to you daily. Humor is a ladder that can take us to a higher place, where we view the world from a more relaxed, positive, creative, joyful, and balanced perspective.

You have added immeasurably to your emotional intelligence with the communication skills you have now learned to develop:

◇ Managing stress
◇ Experiencing and managing your intense emotions
◇ Effectively communicating nonverbally and with emotional intelligence
◇ Bringing a sense of humor into your home and work relationships

These skills have prepared you to redefine your relationship with conflict. The two remaining chapters will help you understand how to sustain meaningful relationships at home and at work by taking conflict in stride, forgiving easily, and not overreacting or underreacting in emotionally charged situations.

# 11 | Conflict Resolution

onflict in relationships can be a deal breaker and a heartbreaker. But resolved conflict can build trust and become a cornerstone for growth in relationships. The way we respond to differences and disagreements in home and work relationships can create hostility and irreparable rifts, or it can initiate the building of safety and trust. That is why conflict is like a *velvet hammer*—an opportunity that can be at once difficult and rewarding. The capacity to take conflict in stride and forgive easily is supported by our ability to manage stress, to be emotionally available, to communicate nonverbally, and to laugh easily.

Painful upset is a part of life. Two people can't possibly always have the same needs, opinions, and expectations. A relationship devoid of challenge stops growing and becomes routine and predictable (maybe even boring), but developing emotionally intelligent communication skills enables you to gracefully overcome relationship challenges.

## Conflict Resolution Requires Both Verbally and Emotionally Intelligent Skills

Successfully resolving differences is essential for the preservation and growth of any relationship. If you can address and resolve conflicts swiftly—without resorting to punishing criticism, contempt, or defensiveness—your relationships will become stronger, and a level of intimacy and trust will develop that can never be obtained without such a test. However, successes and failures hinge on your ability to apply the nonverbal skills that create attuned attachment.

Here are some common examples of people who confront—rather than attend to—conflict *without* using emotionally intelligent communication skills that could bring about successful resolution. These are examples of trying to end conflict by using a hammer without any velvet:

◇ David is a guy everyone loves. He is charming and generous, and he has many admirers, but his irrational rages intimidate friends and family. David's response to disagreement is unpredictable—one minute he seems fine, and the next he is purple with rage and explosive.

- Michelle's responses to disagreements are as sudden and surprising as David's. But instead of heating up, she freezes and withdraws. For days, Michelle will remain silent and icy with those who have inadvertently offended her.

- Claire comes from a family where conflict routinely ended in punishment. She has learned to conceal—even from herself—situations that make her feel frustrated, sad, or frightened. Her goal is to maintain peace and tranquillity in all of her relationships, but Claire's long string of "here today, gone tomorrow" relationships calls into question the wisdom of her belief that the way to win friends and influence others is to avoid conflict altogether.

- Andrea insists that she can deal with conflict in a totally rational manner. But in the heat of the moment, she often loses it and ends up feeling ashamed and embarrassed by behavior she can't seem to control.

## Communication Skills That Help Resolve Conflicts

The attuned relationship bond that originates in infancy creates a template for successful communication in adult relationships. Most of the emotionally intelligent, nonverbal skills developed at that time continue to be benchmarks for resolving conflict. These communication skills include the following:

◇ **The capacity to remain relaxed and focused in tense and intense situations.** If you don't know how to stay centered, relaxed, and in control of yourself, you may become overwhelmed emotionally in challenging situations, such as the following:

The discovery of marijuana in her son's backpack was very stressful for Sandra. Before acting on her impulse to confront him, however, she honed her emotional intelligence by taking a walk to calm herself down and prepared for a conversation rather than an argument. In this more balanced state of mind, she could express to him how upset and worried she was. She listened to his side of things, and together they worked out a plan to deal with his stress and concerns about peer pressure.

◇ **The ability to experience intense emotions and recognize what matters most to you.** If you numb or ignore basic feelings, such as anger, sadness, or fear, you compromise your ability to face and resolve differences. If you fear emotional intensity—yours or someone else's—or insist on exclusively rational outcomes, you will be unable to use the emotional intelligence tools you need to resolve conflicts, such as in the following example:

Michele and Josh were lovers and good friends when something happened that triggered a rush of emotions in Josh. He saw Michele having dinner with another man. Before confronting her, Josh took time to acknowledge to himself the anger and hurt he was feeling. When he subsequently talked with Michele, Josh drew on his emotional intelligence and was honest about his reaction to seeing her with another man. As it turned out, the "other man" was an old friend of Michele's who was in town for the day. Josh's conversations with Michele about his feelings led to a new degree of closeness and intimacy in their relationship.

These kinds of misunderstandings are also very common in work settings. Insecurities pop up all the time, creating wedges between people instead of opportunities to build greater trust.

◆ **The ability to recognize and read nonverbal cues.** As we've seen, the most important information conveyed in relationships often is emotional and nonverbal. It consists of an ongoing interplay that includes eye contact, facial expression, tone of voice, posture, touch, intensity, timing, and pace.

    In personal as well as work relationships, another person's upset may or may not have anything to do with you, but it is good practice to be observant and inquire.

◆ **The capacity to be playful in tense and awkward situations.** Many confrontations can be avoided and differences resolved through the use of humor and reliance on mutual play, such as in the following example:

    Sam is a morning person. When he wakes up, he wants to start his day by being intimate with his new wife. But Judy is a night owl and is groggy in the morning. So Sam gets up, makes coffee, and brings it back to bed, holding it under her nose to wake her up. He playfully cradles her like a child sipping soup while whispering lusty comments in her ear and watching as she warms up in more ways than one.

A note of caution about the use of humor in a conflict: conflict is a trigger for vulnerability that a person may be attempting to hide by posturing. Humor in the presence of vulnerability can be misinterpreted and experienced as contempt. No one likes to be laughed at—it's humiliating and enraging. Your sense of humor is best used first to calm and soothe yourself. You can use humor to put the situation into a more agreeable perspective or to reframe it entirely—for yourself. But if you appear to be laughing at the person you are having a conflict with, you will most assuredly fan the flames of resentment and derail the process of conflict resolution.

These communication skills help resolve conflict in relationships in the following ways:

| | |
|---|---|
| Making it possible to hear others | By not getting emotionally overwhelmed, you can accurately read and interpret verbal and nonverbal communication. |
| Making it possible for others to hear you | When you can both express and control your emotions, you are able to communicate your needs without threatening or punishing others. |
| Aiding in problem solving | By being calm, focused, and emotionally present, you can access the fullest range of information and can negotiate with maximum impact and potentially lasting results. |
| Offering positive alternatives to knee-jerk, disrespectful, and hurtful communication and behavior | Avoiding punishing and degrading words and actions allows people to reunite faster. |
| Building trust | When conflict and disagreement can be worked out quickly and painlessly, trust flourishes. |

# The Influence of Childhood Experiences on Your Reaction to Conflict

The success or failure of your early attachment bond creates expectations about how people will respond to you now. People who grew up believing their needs would be met are resilient and can remain focused, relaxed, and creative in challenging situations. People who grew up without such expectations do not trust themselves or conflict.

What kinds of attachment experiences set the stage for how disagreements will be approached in the future? Let's look at two responses to a similar problem, which demonstrate secure and insecure reactions to differences:

◆ Nat's mother was skilled at understanding her child's needs and resolving differences without shaming or punishing him. He went through periods of rebellion as a toddler and teenager without having to give up on himself or on his parents. There were many disagreements, but they ended in compromises that Nat was able to accept. When he met Toshi, Nat was surprised by the amount of time and attention she asked of him—more than he required, though he deeply loved her. Nat was able to tell Toshi how he felt without humiliating her. In finding a way to address issues that mattered to each of them, their differences were resolved and they grew closer in the process. Nat's flexibility is also apparent in his work relationships. His office staff knows that he will take the time to address their concerns patiently, and this trait has made him an exceptional manager.

◆ Dan's mother had to be hospitalized during his infancy; this upset his father, who took out his anger and frustration on his son. Dan grew up feeling resentful and fearful of conflict. By the time he became an adult, Dan had learned to numb his more vulnerable feelings to the point that he barely recognized them. He also failed to recognize his longing for closeness and tenderness. When he fell in love with Rosario, Dan thought his unhappy past was behind him, but her requests for time, attention, and care overwhelmed and enraged him to the point that resolving their differences became impossible. At work, Dan often found himself in conflict with supervisors and coworkers who made requests from him, and he was likely to snap at them when they interrupted what he was already doing.

*Secure* responses to conflict are characterized by the following:

◆ The capacity to recognize and respond to important matters
◆ A readiness to forgive and forget
◆ The ability to seek compromise and avoid punishing
◆ A belief that resolution can support the interests and needs of both parties

*Insecure* responses to conflict are characterized by the following:

◆ An inability to recognize and respond to matters of great importance to the other person
◆ Explosive, angry, hurtful, and resentful reactions

- The withdrawal of love, resulting in rejection, isolation, shaming, and fear of abandonment
- The expectation of bad outcomes
- The fear and avoidance of conflict

Some of the most difficult conflicts that people with insecure attachment face are with themselves, rather than with those they share a relationship with. Painful and fearful expectations of what *will* happen to them color their perceptions of what *is* happening. For these people, the resolution of their conflict begins with self-inquiry, but it is facilitated by the investment of others who care enough to lend understanding and compassionate support.

## Audrey: The Woman Who Was Used to Feeling Bad About Herself

Audrey's mother was attractive, charming, and funny when sober, but much of the time she was drunk and verbally abusive to her young daughter. Although Audrey's scars weren't physical, they were deep nonetheless—her memories from earliest childhood were of being screamed at and cursed for being "selfish" and "no good." Her stepfather tried to protect Audrey, but there was a limit to what he could do. The day she graduated high school, Audrey left home. Smart, pretty, and hardworking, she found a secretarial job in a large company and began taking night school classes. After earning her degree, she was promoted to a better job in another city. Her new life far from the terrible memories of childhood made her feel safe and happy.

It wasn't long before Audrey met and fell in love with Josh, who was good-looking, charming, and funny. From the beginning, however, there were signs of trouble that

Audrey might have picked up on if she had been more alert. Josh had a relentless need to be on the go, and he seemed unable to relax without having a drink. But Josh didn't get noticeably drunk, so Audrey dismissed what she saw. Once they were married, Josh's dependency on alcohol became more obvious, as did the familiar pattern of living with someone who was cruel—Josh was verbally abusive to Audrey. But she loved him and did her best avoid a divorce . . . until he struck her physically. That ended the marriage.

Heartbroken, Audrey entered therapy to try and understand what had happened and to rebuild her life. Her therapist picked up on Audrey's rigid self-reliance and began helping her rebuild trust in others. The process Audrey invested in made her aware of how tense she often felt and what she could do about it. She also became familiar with her emotions, such as sadness and fear, that she had avoided for so long, and she began experiencing more positive feelings.

During this state of self-discovery, Audrey became aware of Kirk, someone who had always been a part of her social group but whom she had never really noticed before. Kirk was quiet and a little shy around her, but a genuineness about him came through in his warm, engaging smile and the kind expression on his face and in his eyes. When Kirk asked Audrey out, she hesitated because he also told her that he had had a crush on her for a long time—a statement that made Audrey feel uncomfortable, perhaps because she believed him!

Audrey had listed the qualities she was looking for in a man, with "kind, dependable, and interested in me, as well as himself" at the top of her list. Kirk had these qualities. He listened attentively with understanding and anticipated her needs; but oddly, instead of liking the attention, it made her feel extremely uncomfortable. The first time they made love, Audrey felt so tense that she had to ask Kirk to stop.

"Before ending the relationship," Audrey's therapist encouraged, "examine your feelings when you are with Kirk." This led Audrey to the discovery that the very things she wanted were things that frightened her when they did occur: the loving, open way Kirk looked at her, the way he bent down and inclined his head toward her, and even the way he shut off his cell phone when he was with her made Audrey feel apprehensive. "When he is so nice to me, it gives me the creeps and I recoil from his touch," Audrey explained with sadness.

"Why do you suppose Kirk's tenderness elicits such negative reactions from you?" her therapist asked. After a long pause Audrey answered tearfully, "I guess it's because I am afraid his affection for me can't be true. How can Kirk love me when I'm unlovable?" Audrey was so used to feeling something was wrong with her that positive feelings, at first, felt unfamiliar and uncomfortable.

Audrey took what she learned about herself and used it wisely, revealing to Kirk her feelings of self-doubt and self-loathing. Because of her emotional awareness and honesty, Kirk was able to be patient and understanding. It took time before her self-deprecating habits of mind were replaced by a new sense of herself as a worthwhile person, but both she and Kirk persevered.

## Differing Needs Create Challenges for Conflict Resolution

It almost goes without saying that different people require different things to make them feel comfortable and safe. Needs aren't whims—this is so much so that needs create some of the most severe challenges in home and work relationships.

Needs play such a prominent role in our lives:

◆ They are about issues that continue to matter to you, and they stay with you over time.

◆ They support survival and well-being, as they can't be postponed indefinitely without dire consequences.

◆ They continue to fester if ignored, turning up unexpectedly at inappropriate times or in connection with other issues.

◆ They are felt experiences in our bodies, attached to inescapable sensations that create a serious source of stress if ignored.

◆ They have an emotional charge and occupy a place of prominence in your life that sticks with you whether you like them or not.

Differing needs are at the heart of common and serious relationship conflicts, such as in the following examples:

◆ Rosie got along great with her coworkers until she was transferred to a new department. There she was assigned to share office space with Shanaya, and suddenly things went downhill. Rosie liked her environment to be very quiet when she was working, but Shanaya listened to music all day, and it was driving Rosie crazy. She couldn't concentrate and was having trouble getting her work done. Also, Rosie wanted the air conditioner turned up high because she often was too warm, while Shanaya complained that she was freezing.

- Travis has a very large, close family whom he enjoys visiting at least once a year. His wife, Debby, is an only child who enjoys alone time. Travis would like nothing better than to join his family in the reunion they plan every summer, but Debby finds the boisterous crowd of relatives overwhelming.

- Alex's family was casual about walking around in underwear and sharing a bathroom in their small house when he was growing up. His father frequently hugged and kissed his mother in the kitchen, and he could hear them having sex through the thin walls at night. Alex's wife, Tanya, was raised in a family that had much more conservative and reserved attitudes. She is very uncomfortable with Alex's open displays of affection and desire for more unconventional sexual practices.

- Dora grew up in a home of abject poverty, though now she is comfortable financially. She and her husband, Bob, have good-paying jobs with benefits and retirement, but Dora would still rather save money than spend it. Bob wants to enjoy life to the fullest while he can and resents what he perceives as Dora's stinginess.

- Jeff was raised in a relaxed—some would say permissive—environment. Lea came from a home that operated very punctually, with rigidly set mealtimes

and bedtimes. Now that they have a family, sched-
ules and house rules have become an extremely contentious issue between them. When Jeff is late for
dinner, Lea is upset, and Jeff feels that "Lea's rules"
interfere with the relationship he has with his kids.

In relationships, there are also differences when it
comes to the need for safety versus the need for exploration and growth. Everyone needs to feel understood, nur-
tured, and supported, but the ways these needs are met
can vary widely.

In a work setting, this principle is commonly evidenced by the need for safety and predictability versus
the need for freedom to explore new ideas and take risks.
It is acknowledged that both needs have important roles
to play in the long-term success of most businesses—both
deserve respect and consideration.

## How Communication Skills Help Resolve Conflicting Needs

Understanding your own needs helps you better communicate with other people. Adults who are out of touch
with their emotions or are so stressed that they can pay
attention only to some of their emotions won't be able
to understand their own needs. In turn, they also have a
difficult time communicating their feelings to others and
staying on course with what is really troubling them. For
example, couples often argue about petty differences—
the way she hangs the towels, the way he parts his hair—
rather than what is really bothering them.

The abilities to manage stress and to fearlessly experience and express your own emotions enable you to know what you need, as well as what others need. These communication skills help you safely navigate conflict created by opposing needs of other people.

Successful use of the velvet hammer to resolve conflicts depends on the abilities to:

◆ manage stress—be alert and calm
◆ be aware of the emotions that signal needs
◆ be aware and respectful of differences with others

Let's take another look at the previous examples through a lens of emotional intelligence that can identify and express needs:

◆ Rosie and Shanaya are having a problem sharing office space. In the context of each one acknowledging the legitimacy of her own, as well as the other person's, needs, there are limitless possibilities for using the velvet hammer for conflict resolution. Shanaya could use a headset for her music or could see if other kinds of music might be less distracting for her new coworker. Rosie could get a small desk fan for her own comfort, so the room temperature did not have to be so cool. Or perhaps Rosie could get Shanaya a cozy shawl or small space heater as a useful peace offering.

◆ Travis and Debby, who are in deadlock about how to spend their vacation time, might inadvertently bring more emotional charge into their disagreement—with the potential for ongoing hurt feelings. If Travis misunderstands Debby's need for quiet and privacy and instead assumes that she dislikes his family, a painful rift could occur. Fortunately, Travis doesn't try to second-guess Debby when she tells him his family overwhelms her. He accepts what she is telling him and is agreeable to compromise. Hoping that, in time, she will learn to enjoy the chaos of a large family, he willingly agrees to spend one week of their two-week vacation somewhere just with her.

- Alex and Tanya have resolved their conflicts by speaking openly with one another about their differing comfort levels with displays of affection and intimacy. Tanya understands that in spite of her love for him, his ways of being affectionate frighten and overwhelm her. She also understands that he needs to know how much she loves him. Out of this communication came a playful velvet hammer where Tanya and Alex each continue to come up with ways of showing affection and sharing intimacy that they both enjoy.

- Dora and Bob have resolved their money differences by calmly sharing their feelings about the subject. It surprised Dora to realize that Bob, too, linked money to security—but he also needed to enjoy the money he earned, after years of deprivation during his childhood. This other need of Bob's touched Dora, who did not previously know that he also had grown up in poverty. Now, instead of criticizing and calling one another names, such as "stingy" or "spendthrift," Dora and Bob find solutions that make both of them feel safe and secure.

- Jeff and Lea have had a more difficult time resolving their conflict about styles of raising children, because both have so much emotion tied to their own child-hood memories. But the process of working out their differences has brought them closer together. They have attentively conveyed their own feelings and lis-tened to the other's feelings with emotional intel-ligence about what is important to them, and they have been willing to compromise and come up with creative solutions that meet both of their needs.

In personal relationships, a lack of understanding about differing needs can result in distancing, arguments, and breakups. In the work setting, differing needs often lie at the heart of the most bitter disputes. Recognition of the legitimacy of conflicting needs and a willingness to expose them in an environment of compassionate under-standing create opportunities for creative problem solv-ing, team building, and improved relationships.

## When It Is Not Advisable to Attempt Conflict Resolution

Although resolving conflict is beneficial to most relation-ships, it is not beneficial to all relationships, and using the velvet hammer is not advisable in all conflicted sit-uations. It is possible to be involved with someone who threatens, rather than fosters, your survival. When the risk of physical or emotional injury is realistic and ever present, protection and safety always come before rec-onciliation. As long as the threat of harm exists, it will invalidate attempts to reconcile conflict.

In deciding whether you are unsafe, emotionally or physically, consider the following in your relationship:

- Is your physical safety being threatened?
- Are you afraid?
- Are you being beaten down—intellectually or emo-
  tionally—or worn down physically?
- Has your sense of self diminished in the relationship?
- Are you ashamed of the way you are being treated?
- Is the person you have a relationship with unable
  to take responsibility for his or her own injurious
  behavior?
- Does the person you are in a relationship with have
  an alcohol or drug problem?

If you said yes to any of the preceding questions, you
may need assistance before focusing on resolving differences. Talk to a trusted friend, clergy, or a therapist, and
create a plan that ensures your well-being. Conflict resolution cannot be accomplished in an environment where
all people involved do not feel safe. For information about
domestic abuse and violence, call the National Domestic
Violence Hotline at 1-800-799-7233 (1-800-799-SAFE)
or go to helpguide.org on the Internet. If you need help
immediately, call 911.

Fortunately, we can resolve conflicts when we don't
feel threatened, but doing so requires the communication
skills associated with emotional intelligence. The following chapter has more to say about these skills and practices that achieve mutually agreeable resolutions to the
conflicts that inevitably arise in our lives.

# 12 | Strategies for Turning Mad into Glad

Ironically, conflict offers us one of the best opportunities for improving relationships. When conflict ends in resolution, it stimulates brain growth and fosters safety and trust. By learning to tolerate the velvet hammer and avoid overreacting or underreacting in emotionally charged situations, we take control of our emotions, as well as of our ability to be true to ourselves and to the relationships we each care about most.

Conflict or the perception of conflict, which can feel just as real, carries a strong emotional charge. It feels bigger, scarier, and more threatening than most differences because often in addition to the differing needs it addresses, it carries a real or implied element of danger. Although conflict takes effort to negotiate, it is worth the investment we make, because resolving conflict rewards us with stronger, more flexible relationships.

Why do conflicts sometimes feel threatening? Your perception of the danger that conflict poses in important relationships is drawn from memories created in infancy and during early childhood. If your early experiences with conflict in relationships were intimidating and hurtful, you may expect all present-day disagreements to end badly. Painful memories can create a view of conflict in relationships as demoralizing, humiliating, dangerous, and something to fear. If, in addition, your early life experiences left you feeling out of control in your early relationships, conflicts experienced now may even be traumatizing for you.

Conflicts perceived as threatening and overwhelming can trigger fight, flight, or freeze responses, which disable emotional intelligence and any attempts at conflict resolution. When one or both people in a relationship feel unsafe and out of control, the likeliness of their disagreements escalating into conflict grows exponentially. This almost certainly can be the case when neither party has the skills to react in an emotionally intelligent manner.

Disagreements can evolve into conflicts not only in personal relationships but in work relationships as well. Colleagues can start out as friends but end up estranged when fearful expectations are triggered in one or both of them.

## Gil: The Woman Who Won Battles but Lost the War

Gil and Peter were good friends and respected colleagues before she was named CEO and chair of a corporate board. As a board member, Peter had voted enthusiastically for Gil's nomination because in addition to liking her, he thought she had the intelligence and background for the job. But once they began working together, things started to fall apart.

Although Gil was very talented and capable, she was also impatient and unaccustomed to working with strong people who had their own ideas about how things should be done. Plus, because she usually worked spontaneously and quickly, Gil rarely took the time to invite others to join in her decision-making process. As a result, despite the many excellent decisions she made for the company, she alienated members of her board because the decisions were made unilaterally.

At one point, Gil ordered Peter to stop conferring with a disgruntled employee, which was not an unreasonable request. But the demanding and public manner in which she told him made Peter feel as though Gil was trying to control him. His reaction was anger and outrage, blasting Gil during a board meeting. Peter's anger was a hurtful blow to Gil, triggering childhood memories of her father's rages, so her response in defense was also anger. Board meetings thereafter became occasions for shouting matches between the two of them, with the other board members looking on in dismay and disapproval. Before long, Gil was offered a buyout and forced to leave her position in the company, and Peter resigned in disgrace soon after. This was a sad ending to what could have been a wonderful working relationship.

# When Does Conflict Not Feel like a Threat?

The knee-jerk perception of conflict as a threat is much less likely when someone has memories of feeling safe as an infant and young child—even in tense situations. If your memories of discord left you feeling whole and hopeful, you will face new challenges openly and eagerly. Events that have a potential for conflict will seem more adventurous than dangerous. When no threat is felt, conflicts are generally recognized simply as differences that can be resolved.

### Elliot, Who Wouldn't Surrender His Photos

Elliot rarely got into scuffles with others, but when he did, he faced the situations fearlessly. As part of a peace delegation, Elliot was invited to tour the former Soviet Union in 1983 at the height of the Cold War. Travel in Russia was tense at that time and included frequent searches by Soviet police and political posturing by officials. But the Russian people were friendly and gracious. Elliot was invited to a Russian home and served an elaborate dinner, even though he knew the family's financial resources were scarce. The photos that he took that evening of three lively generations living together in one small apartment were precious to him.

The next day Elliot decided to rest at his hotel instead of joining his delegation on a field trip. Later that afternoon, he took a stroll through the neighborhood with his camera. After he stopped to photograph a little boy on a red tricycle, the child disappeared into a long line of people. Immediately the crowd began to complain vigorously about the photo Elliot had just snapped of the little boy. The fuss caused Elliot to remember that he had been expressly told never to photograph people in lines, and he had already witnessed two other delegates' films exposed to light after such an incident.

In the blink of an eye, Elliot found himself between two large policemen who asked him in broken English to give them his camera—something Elliot did not want to do unless it was absolutely necessary. Smiling politely and apologizing, Elliot shoved the camera and its precious film deep into the backpack he held tightly in his arms and pretended he didn't understand what they were asking him. This exchange continued for a few moments as one officer unsuccessfully attempted to call the precinct; then the policemen signaled for Elliot to accompany them to the police station, which turned out to be several miles away. There, he was passed from one group to another, each of apparently higher rank than the last. Finally, there was a phone call to someone who sounded like an official, from the bits of conversation that Elliot understood. He could make out the words, "American, camera," but not much else. At the end of the call, the men shrugged, smiled sheepishly, and indicated that Elliot was free to go.

When Elliot described what had happened to the other members of his delegation, they asked him why he didn't immediately hand over the film. His answer was, "If they had threatened me, I would have. If the demands sounded aggressive or anyone laid a hand on me, I would have given in. But that didn't happen, so I held my ground."

## Developing the Ability to Resolve Conflict

People respond differently to discord depending on what they expect to experience. If we anticipate hurt or humiliation, we approach the situation with fear and trepidation. When our expectation is positive, the same situation becomes an opportunity to improve our relationships. This explains why Elliot's response to a potentially threatening situation was so different than Gil's . . . but it doesn't explain why Elliot responded as he did.

There are two possible reasons for Elliot's response. The first is that he grew up in a home where disputes ended amiably instead of being the terrifying events they were for Gil. The second is that Elliot learned to behave in the calm, friendly, fearless way he did because as an adult he learned emotionally intelligent skills that enabled him to do the following:

- Quickly reduce his stress levels
- Experience and manage his strong emotions
- Recognize and practice nonverbal communication
- Meet challenges with a sense of humor

These four skills together form a fifth skill that is greater than the sum of its parts: the ability to take conflict in stride and resolve differences in ways that build trust and confidence. In situations that could feel threatening, this skill gives you the power to do the following:

- **Stay focused in the present.** Focusing on the present, untainted by fear from the past, opens up new possibilities for resolving not only current but also past disputes. Time changes the way people feel, think, and act. When we are emotionally present and not holding on to old hurts and resentments, we can recognize the reality of a current situation and view it as a new opportunity for resolving old feelings about conflicts. We can even use these opportunities to revive and revitalize relationships that were cherished but lost.

- **Choose your arguments.** Developing skills that make us emotionally intelligent nonverbal communicators takes time. They are not accomplished through speedy electronic processes. Because arguments require an expenditure of time and energy, we need to consider what is worth arguing about and what is not. Maybe we don't want to surrender a parking space if we have already been around the block three times looking for a place to park. But if there are dozens of empty spaces elsewhere in a parking structure, arguing over a single space isn't worth the energy.

- **Forgive.** It's much easier to be compassionate and forgive when we don't feel threatened and have taken the time to listen and understand. But it is harder to pardon or forget when injuries continue to be inflicted. The process of forgiveness begins by assessing whether or not the hurtful treatment continues in the present. If it does, it's up to us to protect ourselves from harm. Resolution lies in releasing the urge to punish, which can never compensate for our losses and only adds to our injury by further depleting and draining our lives.

◊ **End conflicts that can't be resolved.** It takes two people to keep an argument going. Again, if we have no realistic reason to fear the person we are arguing with, we should be able to disengage from the conflict, if we choose. Whether or not we can do this effectively depends on our ability to understand the other person's complaints without becoming defensive. A story always has more than one side. The ability to see the other person's point of view as well as our own removes the tendency to become self-righteous or to justify ourselves, enabling us to disengage without becoming further drained.

## Stress Reduction Leads the Way to Conflict Resolution

Primary skills turn potential conflicts into opportunities. The primary skills of stress reduction and emotional management play a pivotal role in conflict resolution by setting the stage for the effective use of humor and nonverbal communication. They also inform the critical part of conflict resolution that involves an awareness of our own emotions and needs, as well as those of others. These skills, which are so fundamental to the attachment process, were examined in the first half of this book. Without them, we would lack the means for turning challenging and potentially threatening experiences into opportunities for growth and development.

The upset of an unexpected clash with someone we care about is enough to trigger a stress response in most people. If we become overwhelmed or underwhelmed, the dispute is much more likely to go unresolved, with little chance of the relationship ending up in a better place than it started.

The first thing to ask yourself when someone upsets you is, "Do I feel threatened?" If the answer is yes, you may want to assess your stress level before doing anything else. Do you detect an overactive fight response, an underactive flight response, or the anxious alert state that signals a freeze response? Any of these responses signal that you are overwhelmed, which can trump your ability to think and behave at your best.

Here is a brief exercise to help you quickly assess your stress level at the beginning of any confrontation.

### Exercise: Am I Having a Traumatic Response to This Confrontation?

These questions can be written on stickers and placed on your desk, in your car, around the house, and anywhere else where you might need to be reminded to be more aware of your responses during difficult situations.

- Fight response: Is my foot on the gas? Do I feel angrier than the situation warrants?
- Flight response: Is my foot on the brake? Am I spacing out? Do I feel in a daze?
- Freeze response: Is my foot on both the gas and the brake? Do I feel frozen, paralyzed, and agitated?
- Do I feel threatened? Do I expect to be punished, hurt, or humiliated in some way?
- Do I feel out of control? Do I feel unable to effectively state my case or defend myself?

When you answer yes to any of these questions, take a time-out until you feel less stressed. Something as simple as taking several slow, deep breaths or lightly tapping your head with your fingertips can restore balance if you are agitated. In addition, you can use the understanding and practices in Chapter 3 and Chapter 4 to immediately calm and focus yourself. By reducing stress, you not only diminish apprehension but also become more aware of your feelings and needs.

## Janette: The Woman Who Was Afraid to Confront Her Mother

Janette was the mother of a ten-month-old son and a three-year-old daughter when she was first diagnosed with breast cancer. Determined to do everything she could to prolong her life, she went into psychotherapy, because she suspected that stress played a role in her illness. In spite of her close and supportive relationships with her husband, close friends, and family, Janette often found herself upset and angry.

As Janette explored her relationships in greater detail, her therapist noticed a shift taking place whenever Janette talked about her mother, Grace. Janette described the relationship as very supportive, especially now, as she underwent chemotherapy. She appreciated her mother's help with the children and household chores. Janette spoke lovingly of Grace, but as she talked, her body language and breathing changed: her jaw stiffened, her shoulders lifted, the tone of her voice became higher, and her breathing became shallow. Observing these changes, the therapist asked Janette to stop for a moment and take a few deep breaths before continuing. Then the therapist asked Janette to describe what she was feeling when she talked about her mother.

Janette answered in a surprised tone of voice, "I guess I feel tense."

"What do you feel emotionally?" her therapist asked, reminding her to take a few more slow, deep breaths before answering the question.

"Maybe a little angry. But why should I be angry with my mother?"

"I don't know," her therapist answered, "but few people have no flaws whatsoever."

By taking time to make sure she was relaxed, Janette could identify her troubled feelings about her relationship with her mother: "I'm a grown woman with two children of my own, and I don't want to be told how to manage my marriage, my children, and my household."

Janette decided that to rid herself of the burden of stress caused by her mother's intrusiveness, she had to tell her mother how she felt and ask for some changes in their relationship. But the prospect of doing this terrified her. Janette was certain that what she had to say would upset her mother—someone she not only loved but very much needed at this time in her life. So she used the relaxation techniques she practiced in therapy before having a discussion with her mom. As a result, those techniques helped her stay connected to her feelings and her need for a different kind of relationship. Pausing frequently to make sure she wasn't tightening up, Janette fully explained to her mother how she felt.

Although Grace was taken aback, she listened to her daughter and promised to restrain her opinions in the future. Grace wasn't able to change a lifetime of habits at all times, but that didn't matter to Janette, because she now felt comfortable to speak up whenever she was irritated. Ultimately, her affection for her mom grew, not only because her mother listened when it must have been difficult to do so, but also because it had been very stressful and draining for Janette to bottle up her irritation.

## Nonverbal, Emotionally Intelligent Communication Builds Trust

When stress is under control, we are more aware of our emotional needs and can better access nonverbal modes of communication, which are powerful tools for resolving conflicts in ways that build trust.

Words spoken in the heat of anger rarely communicate the real issues at play in a dispute. Dialogue in heated confrontations is more likely to serve a protective, rather than communicative, role. Conversely, unspoken, emotionally intelligent communication can say more than the deliberately hurtful words uttered in emotionally charged situations. The fact that Elliot didn't speak Russian was probably an advantage during his dispute with the Russian police officers, because it forced him to pay attention to their nonverbal signals. Had he picked up hostile, aggressive signals in the officers' facial expressions, tone of voice, gestures, or body language, he would not have felt safe to defy their orders to surrender his camera. Although conflict with strangers is apt to be less threatening than conflict with someone we know well, fortunately nonverbal communication skills work even better with people whom we care about.

### Trish and Andrea: Face-to-Face

Trish and Andrea enjoyed a good relationship as business partners until Andrea began to feel victimized by the amount of time she needed to devote to a project. Overwhelmed by the prospect of what lay ahead, she sent Trish an e-mail demanding a larger share of the profits. Trish was shocked and hurt by the message and by the impersonal way it was delivered. Rather than let herself become overwhelmed by hurt and disappointment, she reminded herself that she and Andrea were friends and that she didn't understand what was so troubling. Trish made an appointment to discuss the matter leisurely with Andrea in a comfortable setting that favored communication.

When the two met, Trish was relaxed and genuinely interested in knowing why Andrea felt resentful when she hadn't in the past. Face-to-face, with Trish showing genuine interest and regard, Andrea relaxed and was able to tell Trish that their project had become more than she could handle. Andrea felt reassured by Trish's support and their interaction, as they discussed possible solutions that would enable Andrea to continue working on the project. The discussion ended with each feeling greater excitement about working together and more appreciation for one another.

## Emotionally Intelligent Communication Cues That Help Resolve a Conflict

Nonverbal, emotionally intelligent communication is, more often than not, responsible for success or failure in conflict resolution. When one person gives the impression of being angry or defensive, it triggers defensiveness in the other person. A clenched jaw, distressed lines around the eyes, or raised shoulders can and most likely will invite fear and opposition. In intense emotional situations, it is not the words that have the most power to sway, but the nonverbal communication. By eliminating stress and being able to focus on reading the cues you are giving others, or they are giving you, conflicts can be resolved more quickly and easily.

Here are some questions to ask yourself about emotionally intelligent, nonverbal communication when you are in conflict:

◇ Do the spoken words align with the expressed nonverbal signals and body language? Does the person I

am facing look more upset or less upset than his or
her words convey?

◆ Do the spoken words strike me as sincere or as
attempts at manipulation? People who are fearful
posture more than those who are unafraid.

◆ Do I detect fearfulness or defensiveness in the nonverbal cues I hear, see, and feel? For example, does
the other person refuse to make eye contact with
me?

◆ How congruent am I? Does what I am saying convey
what I am feeling? Am I asking for what I need?

## Listening Is the Healing Heart of Conflict Resolution

Listening is the real art in diplomacy and negotiation
because the words people use when they are upset rarely
convey the issues and needs at the heart of their problems. Good listeners watch to see that the spoken words
correspond with the unspoken communication. When
we listen for what is felt as well as said, we connect more
deeply to our own needs and emotions, and to those of
other people. Listening in this way also strengthens us,
informs us, and makes it easier for others to hear us.

### Greg: The Man Who Moved Mountains with His Ears

People with mental illness face a further handicap of having an unrealistic stigma associated with their mental
problems. Generations of B horror movies have planted

fear in people's minds about mental illness. As the director of a mental health facility, Greg faced the challenge of this negative perception when he was looking for space to permanently house sixty-five mentally ill occupants. After years of searching, an affordable building was found in a partially residential neighborhood. The biggest problem with getting the project off the ground was acquiring the necessary approval by the city council. Neighbors were organizing a campaign to speak out against the development when it came up for a council vote.

Greg knew it would be an uphill battle to convince the neighbors that the project actually would be good for their neighborhood and represented no risk to them. He expected his job to be difficult because the neighbors felt threatened and he understood the depth of people's fears. In Greg's experience, no matter what he said or did, some people would never be swayed from their fearful view of those who are mentally ill. He also knew that while a few of the neighbors were already behind the project, the vast majority felt conflicted about it. To gain the support of this large group of people, Greg had to do more than simply understand their concerns; he had to address them as well.

Meeting with them and listening to their points of view was a time-consuming process, but well worth the effort. By hearing the people's apprehensions and addressing them, Greg also had a chance to describe the benefits of the project and its safety precautions. When the building was finally approved and built, the neighbors not only liked it but also felt safe enough to frequent the thrift shop and mini-mart run by community members. In time, a close and supportive relationship developed among the new and the established members of the neighborhood.

## Becoming a More Effective Listener

When we are quarreling with someone, it is wise to listen until we understand the other person's real concerns and they acknowledge feeling that they are truly being heard. Listening gives everyone involved an opportunity to make a contribution to the solution of a problem. This therapeutic process can result in reconciliation and healing.

To resolve a conflict by being an effective listener, it's important to try to understand why the other person is really upset:

- Listen to the reasons the other person gives for being upset.
- Make sure you understand what the other person is telling you—from his or her point of view.
- Repeat the other person's words, and ask if you have understood correctly.
- Ask if anything remains unspoken, giving the person time to think before answering.
- Resist the temptation to interject your own point of view until the other person has said everything he or she wants to say and feels that you have listened to and understood his or her message.

The velvet hammer is an extraordinarily powerful emotionally intelligent skill that gives us the ability to grow and change safely within our relationships. Composed of other skills that give it force and flexibility, fearlessly facing and resolving conflict without compromising ourselves is the key to sustaining long-lasting relationships. No relationship thrives for long when conflicts can't be resolved in ways that improve connection. Resentment, bitterness, discontent, and disappointment, spoken or unspoken, will infect the quality of our relationships, making them toxic. No skill is more necessary for the health, well-being, and longevity of our relationships than the ability to resolve conflict.

# Conclusion
## Preserving Positive Change in Your Life

Congratulations! If you have come this far and read all or most of the material, give yourself a pat on the back. And if you actually practiced the longer exercises in Chapter 4 and Chapter 6, give yourself a big hand of applause. This isn't a book just about emotional intelligence; it's a book about how to change lifelong habits by changing your mind and your brain. But one more thing still needs to happen before your brain, behavior, and emotional reality remain changed.

To ensure that what you have learned sticks, you need to practice. How long this is necessary depends on the consistency of your practice. If you practice daily for a month or two, that may be enough to achieve the results you have in mind. If you practice less consistently, you will make less progress. Some of this may sound difficult, but in fact it isn't. It's actually fun, because the rewards for using emotionally intelligent communication are immediate and powerful.

Unfortunately, if you don't have a plan for implementing the skills you have learned, chances are that you will forget to use them. Now that you have a blueprint, however, your odds for success are great if you personalize it to meet your own individual needs.

Here are some questions to consider as you formulate a personal plan for making emotionally intelligent communication a permanent part of your life:

◆ **What is your plan? Exactly how will you continue to use the nonverbal skills you have learned?** Your daily interactions with other people offer unlimited opportunities for being aware of how you communicate nonverbally and where the skills you have learned can be applied to improve and enhance your connections with others. Take advantage of every opportunity you get by being aware of how you communicate with others and observing how different nonverbal communication techniques enhance those interactions.

Planned practice sessions of the exercises you have learned will provide increased improvements in your relationships with people who are as willing and eager as you to create a new level of trust and connection.

◆ **With whom will you practice your new skills?** This may seem like a difficult question to answer, but it really isn't.

During casual interactions of daily life, you can be practicing at all times with unwitting participants. Notice how people react differently to you when you make changes or adjustments in the ways you approach or interact with them. Notice the satisfaction you feel when these small changes make your daily activities more pleasant and satisfying.

Approach potential practice session partners with a positive attitude; most people want and need to become better communicators. Family members, friends, colleagues, and acquaintances may be more interested than you realize in exploring, listening, and participating in practices that are mutually beneficial. Consider whether or not the person you are thinking of pairing up with is a good listener or not. If you ask questions and demonstrate interest, people will want to be with you.

◆ **Where will you practice these skills?** Will you practice at home, at work, or when relaxing with friends? Are some environments better or safer to practice in than others? Are some environments more private, less chaotic, and more secure than others?

When engaging in planned practice sessions, you don't want to be interrupted. Agree upon some basic guidelines, such as turning off phones and ignoring computers so you won't be distracted by electronic gadgetry. Select a setting or location where other distractions will be kept to a minimum.

◆ **When will you practice the skills you have learned? What time can you make available for practice? How will you structure your time?** We have opportunities every day to be with people and communicate with them nonverbally. Encounters with those who are young and old, familiar and unfamiliar—all give us a chance to speak out nonverbally in the way we look, listen, and react to them.

If you are concerned about finding time for planned practice sessions, revisit the Introduction, which discusses your use of time, and you will be reminded of how much time is wasted on unrewarding activities.

During planned practice sessions, take approximately thirty minutes to focus on communicating nonverbally and verbally what you feel about yourself, the relationship, or the work you are doing together. Pay close attention to your own momentary physical sensations and emotions, as well as the nonverbal cues being conveyed by the other person.

Ideally, it would be most beneficial to initially carve out a regular time—preferably five or six days a week—to schedule at-home or at-work thirty-minute sessions. This commitment to change in the beginning can result in dramatic improvements in your most important relationships.

◆ **How can you make what you have learned a lasting part of your life? What parts of your life provide the best opportunities for integrating emotionally intelligent communication? Can you make these existing settings more conducive to in-depth communication?** Consider multitasking. In addition to applying the skills you have learned to everyday activities, pair up with a friend, loved one, or colleague to practice while doing something that is already a habit, such as taking a walk or having a meal. Remember, learning won't take place when you are exhausted; you have to be calm and alert to learn. By keeping your stress from interfering with your ability to be "present" and "connected" to other people, you will be more open to genuine interactions that can dramatically improve your relationships.

Emotionally intelligent communication helps us be great communicators, but more than that, it enables us to create the quality of life we want, need, and deserve. Emotionally intelligent nonverbal communication keeps us focused in the present, alert to opportunity as well as danger, and receptive to joyous connections with other people, but it's not magic. It's a birthright that we can develop at any time in our lives. As surely as we know that stem cells exist in the most emotional part of the brain, we know that change for the better is possible. We all have what it takes if we are willing to apply ourselves.

# Index